The View from Sunset Boulevard

THE VIEW FROM SUNSET BOULEVARD

AMERICA AS BROUGHT TO
YOU BY THE PEOPLE
WHO MAKE TELEVISION

BEN STEIN

Basic Books, Inc., Publishers   *New York*

Library of Congress Cataloging in Publication Data

Stein, Benjamin, 1944–
  View from Sunset Boulevard.

  Includes index.
    1. Television broadcasting—United States.
  2. Television broadcasting—Social aspects—United
  States.   3.   Television programs—United States.
  I. Title.
  HE8700.8.S83   791.45'0973   78-54999
  ISBN: 0-465-09032-X

For My Father

CONTENTS

Contents

Contents viii

INTRODUCTION

~~~~~~~~ $\mathbf{B}$ECAUSE this book deals with a sensitive subject, its origins deserve to be explained. In 1969 and 1970, while I was a student at Yale Law School, I was privileged to take a course in film from Stanley Kauffmann, a well-known and intelligent critic who regularly traveled the disgusting railroad run from New York to New Haven to fill our heads with the lore of the cinema. Just what the focus of the class was supposed to have been I do not know. I do know that Professor Kauffmann assigned to us the reading of Siegfried Kracauer's *From Caligari to Hitler,* the famous study of films in Weimar Germany.

For me, it was like opening Chapman's *Homer.* Instead of repeating vague nonsense about "pacing," "personality," and other words which have no meaning in that context, Kracauer talked about the relation of films to real life. He explained, in a convincing and analytical way, how the films of Weimar revealed the social and political thinking of a neurotic nation. The analyses were brilliant and thoroughly impressive. There, I thought, was the meat of film study.

Almost immediately, I discovered that the techniques of law school study—the rigorous analysis and lining up of similar and dissimilar cases to attempt to explain why a decision went a certain way—those techniques which were so boring in law school could be brought to bear on film study with useful results.

The first film I tried it on was *The Bicycle Thief,* in which I thought I saw the remnants of syndicalism and corporatism, even though it was made after World War II in supposed reaction to Mussolini. Professor Kauffmann, a generous man, complimented me lavishly on my efforts and results (while a fellow student, from the Yale Drama School, told me that I "think too much").

When I left law school to enter the drab world of legal practice in Washington, D.C., I scrounged a job at American University, teaching part-time about the political and social content of film. I also taught the same thing for three quarters at the University of California at Santa Cruz, during a hiatus in the practice of trade regulation law.

Santa Cruz, nestled in the redwoods on mountains sloping down to the Pacific, could hardly be a more beautiful town. But there is little to do there. So, for the first time in my life, I started to watch a lot of television. It was a revelation. In the midst of the most inane and repetitious television shows, comedy and adventure, and even soap operas, there was a spate of political and social messages so clear and interesting that they would have made Kracauer pass out with joy.

The messages were deeply similar, or so it seemed to me. Businessmen were bad people and workers were good people. High-level police were bad people, representative of a rotten and deadening bureaucracy, and idiosyncratic, rebel cops were the salt of the earth and smart, too. This said something about organizations and bureaucracies, and about the value of rebellion as com-

pared with acceptance. It spoke to questions of confor-
mity and satisfaction with society.

Small towns were superficially lovely, but under a thin
veneer of cornpone there was lurking, terrifying evil, waiting to ensnare the innocent Natty Bumppo of the big city.
But big cities, at first glance jungles where narcotics
dealers disguised as real estate salesmen lurked on every
corner, offering heroin and white slavery to small children,
were basically friendly, cheerful places. Only in the suburbs was there sanctuary, but even there, in the white
frame house behind the picket fence, surrounded by
emerald lawns, lurked Mr. Big of the syndicate, paying for
his daughter's trip to Europe with the agony of the junkie.
This, too, told something about the geography of
America's desires, the locus of happiness and serenity in
America. And it all happened with such consistency that I
could not but marvel at the way TV shows resembled re-
curring dreams and nightmares, just as Kracauer had
marveled at the repetition of genres in Germany long
ago.

After a decent interval of mortification, I began to write
about television and other popular cultural subjects for
the *Wall Street Journal*. My columns, such as they were,
generally did not say whether a show was good or bad
but reported instead on its artifactual value, as Kracauer
had done. Still further along, I spent a month in Hollywood (courtesy of the *Wall Street Journal*) hanging
around at Norman Lear's Tandem/TAT studio, sitting
for day after day in the office of Al Burton, Lear's genial
and brilliant Vice President for Creative Affairs. I noticed
two amazing things. First, Lear, Burton, and the other
people at Tandem were the finest, most thoughtful people I had ever met. Second, the people who made all

those TV shows, the writers and the producers, believed all the things that were being illustrated on television. The specters of television were the beliefs of the men and women who wrote and produced the shows. (In television, unlike in the movies, directors are creatively trivial factors, as are actors and actresses. Writers and producers are the real creative force.

I noticed further that the lives of men and women and children on TV shows, so different from any life I had ever seen or participated in, was really the life of Los Angeles—the clean streets; the polite, handsome police; the shiny new cars issued to everyone over sixteen; the strong-jawed men and the lean, unthreatening women; the tinkling of glasses around a swimming pool; the pastel hues of storefronts; the dark, richly upholstered restaurant interiors; the squealing of tires along canyon roads; and much more.

In an article about my stay in Los Angeles, I said that the city was the original in the giant Xerox machine of television, as I believe it is. The social critic Irving Kristol, then a kindly editor at Basic Books, read my article and asked me if I wanted to expand that concept into a book. Since I wanted to leave New York and move to Los Angeles, I readily agreed.

I came to Los Angeles and worked on various projects for about a year. Some of them involved constant work at a TV production company for the whole year. In that time I tried to learn as much as possible about the social and political thoughts of those men and women who created TV shows.

My theory was that television is the dominant communications mode in America, that it is sending out messages of great potency, and that it would be wonderful to know as much about the messages—and the senders of the messages—as possible. It is a simple idea, but one with an undeniable appeal.

I also arranged to interview in person and by proxy about forty important TV writers and producers. I asked them a set of questions designed to draw out their feelings about American life. (I also interviewed a few movie producers, but only a few. Movies, I think, have become largely a phenomenon of a single, fairly small class, whose messages—while interesting—reach a miniscule fraction of the numbers that television reaches. Also, on a personal level, it was extremely difficult to see movie producers and writers.)

When I examined what people had told me about life in those interviews, I discovered what I thought I would discover, which was that the homogeneity of the views of television's creative people is almost uncanny. Moreover, in several years of extremely concentrated exposure to television, I learned that the product is extremely homogeneous as well. And the fit between the message of the TV shows and the opinions of the people who make the TV shows was excellent. Moreover, the views of these TV people were so highly idiosyncratic and unique that they could not possibly be the dreams of a nation. It was like thinking that a taste for snuff movies or Beluga caviar was the general taste of a nation.

All of this means something elementary but interesting. The super-medium of television is spewing out the messages of a few writers and producers (literally in the low hundreds), almost all of whom live in Los Angeles. Television is not necessarily a mirror of anything besides what those few people think. The whole entertainment component of television is dominated by men and women who have a unified, idiosyncratic view of life. When a viewer understands that television is not supposed to be a facsimile of life but instead is what a Hollywood producer thinks life is, the viewer can then understand the match or mismatch between television and what he knows to be true.

A few further cautionary words. Before I started to write this book, a good and talented friend, John Gregory Dunne, told me that some people might regard it as a witch hunt and others might find it strange that the subject needed to be examined at all. I cannot say anything helpful to the second group. The book is certainly not a witch hunt, since, as the reader will discover, the people whose views and product I have explored are fine people whose life and work I admire greatly and to whose ranks I aspire. I do not agree with much of what they see as reality, but I was never convinced that I had a monopoly on understanding reality.

This book does not purport to be either exhaustive or scientific. Because of the limits of time and ability and money, I could not study all the shows or people I wanted to study. Considering how few active producers and writers there are, I think I have talked to enough to have at least an idea of what is on their minds. I do not claim that I have touched every base. Again, because of the limits of my ability and means, the book is far less historical than I wanted it to be. Had I but money enough and time, I would have studied the writers, directors, and producers who survive from the earliest days of the movies and television. That, unfortunately, was simply a bigger exercise than I could manage. So what I have recorded is basically a moment—the mid- and late seventies—set out in time with only a brief historical preamble. And, finally, I would consider this book and the writing of it wasted if it were not read with the same love for the people of Hollywood that I have felt since I got here. Among the people I talked to for this book are the finest people alive.

The View from Sunset Boulevard

CHAPTER ONE

The Making of a TV Show

🎶🎶🎶 **W**HEN a viewer turns on his television, he sees the end product of a long and complicated process that bounces ideas, money, people, and equipment around the country for months (and sometimes years) before a show is finally "in the can." For prime-time television, the shows that appear on the three networks in the three most heavily watched hours of each day, usually eight P.M. to eleven P.M., the process is especially serious and freighted with complications, since so much money is involved. That "Baretta" episode the viewer barely sees while talking on the telephone is the culmination of the deep thought and consideration of many highly-paid people. The troubles of Indianapolis divorcée Anne Romano and her two teenage daughters, Barbara and Julie, trivial as they may seem on "One Day At A Time," have engaged hundreds of thousands (and sometimes millions) of dollars worth of creative time.

The process of making a show usually begins in Los Angeles, with one of the many TV production companies, for TV shows are hardly ever made by the networks themselves—at least for prime time. Rather, a group of TV show contractors is responsible. In the summer of 1976 there were fewer than a dozen contractors of any size. The biggest is Universal, the TV arm of MCA, Inc., which specializes in adventure shows. The two comedy giants, MTM (run by Mary Tyler Moore's husband, Grant Tinker) and Tandem/TAT, Norman Lear's operation, come next in terms of output.

After that come the TV production divisions of the formerly huge motion picture studios—M-G-M, Twentieth Century Fox, and Paramount. Paramount, which now has two smash hit comedies, "Laverne & Shirley" and "Happy Days," is especially "hot" as this is being written. Two action adventure companies, Quinn Martin Productions and Spelling/Goldberg, are also highly productive. Then there are several smaller outfits making comedies, such as Komack, Punkin, and TOY (an acronym for Turtletaub, Orenstein, and Yorkin). There are many others, but these are the main producers of prime-time television. All are located in Los Angeles.

The process of getting an idea made into a show varies, but in general it goes something like this. A network programming executive will let the word get out that he thinks his network needs, let us imagine, more situation comedy with a new look. This message floats around Los Angeles, and producers and writers try to think of situation comedies (sitcoms) that will fill the bill.

A producer in a company like Tandem/TAT may come up with something, which he then brings to Norman Lear as an oral presentation. If the idea is pleasing to Lear, he may request a written "treatment" of the concept. That means a description of the show and its characters, along with an outline of how the first few episodes would go.

If the written presentation is still attractive, Lear might then send it to a network with a request that the network pay for a script based on the treatment. If the programming people approve, the network will pick up the cost of the treatment, which Lear has already advanced, as well as the cost of the script, which might be more than $20,000 for a 22-minute pilot.

The script, if approved by Lear, then goes to the network, and the people there brood about it. If they like it, they can authorize the making of a pilot. At this point actors, actresses, and directors are discussed. Occasionally a network will have a particular performer under contract to appear in something as yet undefined which the network is to air. The networks do not like to throw this "holding money" away, so, other things being equal, they will pick from among those so held.

A producer and writers will also be discussed, because no one person ever writes a TV show. That simply does not happen. All shows are rewritten over and over again, and the networks like to know who the rewriters are, although this is a far smaller concern than who the performers will be.

At this point, if network and production company people can agree on everything, the production goes forward. A single episode is made, usually at a cost of at least $150,000 for a half-hour show, and the videotape is sent to the network.

The network is free to like or dislike the project. Most projects will be rejected. If the network likes the show, it may order an additional number up to thirteen. At that point, the show becomes a going concern, and, while a network representative attends tapings and (rarely) some story conferences, the production company is largely left to its own devices in making the show.

Since we are interested in how the Los Angeles community of writers and producers translates its political, cultural, and social views into TV shows, it is good to note that almost all of the creative content of TV shows, even at the earliest stages, comes from these Los Angeles folk. It is true that the networks make the final selection of TV fare, but they select from a menu that has been drawn up in Hollywood.

It is likewise correct that the process of selection from idea to ongoing TV show is like going through the eye of a needle. Al Burton of Tandem/TAT estimates that out of twenty ideas good enough for scripts to be made, eight will get to be pilots and two will become series. But again, all of those that make it, as well as those that do not, come from the same group of producers and writers.

This means that we do not need to go outside of the small group of Los Angeles writers and producers to find out about the people whose conscious and unconscious attitudes go into our TV shows.

And the group is small indeed. There are thousands of members of the Writers' Guild, the wonderful union to whose meetings the members regularly ride in Rolls Royces. But only around two hundred writers (and this includes producers, most of whom started as writers) work steadily in comedy, and an even smaller number work consistently in adventure shows.

It is much as if the entire content of the prime-time TV hopper were fabricated by the residents of one of America's smallest towns. Everyone knows everyone else, and, also as in small towns, everyone looks like everyone else. And everyone knows what everyone else is doing.

Everyone also knows what everyone else thinks. But before examining that, it might be worthwhile to see just what is on television these days.

CHAPTER TWO

The Top Shows

𝔒𝔰𝔒𝔰𝔒𝔰 T ELEVISION, circa May,
1977, consists of several forms of varying duration. There
are sports events, movies, movies made for television, variety shows, "specials," and an occasional news show.
But the most durable forms are the situation comedy and
the adventure show. Of the top twenty shows (in terms of
viewer popularity) in May 1977, ten are continuing sitcoms or adventure shows. Twenty-four of the top forty
are sitcoms or adventure shows. If movies made expressly for television are added, sixteen of the top twenty
shows were made up of entertainment fiction made by
the Los Angeles production community. Thirty-four of
the top forty shows are so created.

And within those numbers are interesting data. Sitcoms
are far and away the dominant mode of top-twenty
shows. There are eight of them versus only two adventure shows (one of which is "Charlie's Angels"—more of
a soft-core pornographic movie than anything else) in the
top twenty. In the next twenty, on the other hand, adventure shows are more numerous than sitcoms, but only by
a small margin.

Contrary to what some may remember about television long ago, there were no westerns on television as
continuing series. There were no shows of any kind de-

picting a full, contemporary, contented family—mother,
father, and children—in a middle-class situation.

In the situation comedies in the top twenty, the following formats were in use:

M.A.S.H.—the high jinks of some lovable physicians in a mobile army surgical hospital stationed behind the lines during the Korean War;
Laverne & Shirley—the lovable high jinks of two young working-class women who work in a brewery in Milwaukee
during the late 1950s;
One Day At A Time—the lovable high jinks of a middle-aged
(but young-looking) divorcée in Indianapolis living with
her two sex bomb teenage daughters, set in the present;
Happy Days—in which "the Fonz," a friendly hard guy, and
a happy middle-class family in a small midwestern town in
the late 1950s have many lovable high jinks;
Barney Miller—the present-day adventures of a group of
lovable beaten-down policemen in a beaten-down pre-
cinct house in New York City, lovably coping with crime;
Welcome Back, Kotter—in which a former student at a Brook-
lyn high school (when it was predominantly Jewish) re-
turns as a lovable teacher when the school's student body
is mostly black and Puerto Rican, set in the present;
All in the Family—about America's favorite lovable bigot, Archie Bunker, and his family in a lower middle-class neigh-
borhood in Queens, set in the present;
What's Happening—the exciting travails of a group of lovable
poor, black teenagers in a big cheerful, city ghetto, set in
the present.

In the second twenty, the situation comedies run along
the following lines:

Alice—the adventures of a divorcée with a small child working
in a truck-stop café in the southwestern United States, set
in the present;

Good Times—the trials and tribulations of a black family
headed by a widowed former maid, living in a public
housing project but too proud and resourceful to take welfare, set in Chicago in the present time;
Hollywood High—the exciting adventures of a group of four
contemporary high school students right at the corner of
Sunset and Highland, set in the present.

In the top ten of the adventure category for May 1977,
there were:

Charlie's Angels—the erotic and crime-fighting exploits of three
glamorous women working for a private detective agency,
set in Los Angeles in the present time;
Streets of San Francisco—an older cop and a younger cop
fighting criminals in present-day San Francisco.

In the second twenty, there were far more adventure
shows:

Kojak—the famous bald-headed New York City detective of
Balkan extraction working within the police department of
Gotham in the present day;
Barnaby Jones—an aging detective prowling southern Califor-
nia in search of criminals in the present day;
Police Story—in which different characters each week face per-
sonal and criminal problems on the beat, set in Los
Angeles of the moment;
Columbo—how an eccentric police detective sheepishly
worms the truth out of invariably rich and powerful felons
in Los Angeles of the present day;
Hawaii-Five-O—several detectives in the Hawaii police force
trying to keep crime under control in beautiful settings in
the lush islands, set in the present;
Starsky and Hutch—in which two policemen, one blond, the
other dark, mete out brutal justice to thugs in the San
Francisco area in the present day.

So far as can be learned, there is no ideological or cultural reason for the preponderance of adventure shows set in Los Angeles. Pure economics dictates that outdoor shooting be done in Los Angeles. Taking a show to another city, even a West Coast city like San Francisco, can raise production costs per episode by more than 50 percent. (One of the best TV shows ever made, "Harry O," was set in San Diego. Although the ratings were adequate by most standards, they were not high enough to offset the extra costs of shooting, even in the large city closest to Los Angeles, so the show went off the air.)

Interior shots for almost all shows are taken in Los Angeles. Some say that applies even to "Kojak" and "Streets of San Francisco." Comedies are photographed or videotaped entirely indoors, in studios in Los Angeles. A few establishing shots will be taken in the city where the comedy is supposed to take place long before the first show airs, and then the shows themselves are made within sound stages.

An attempt is made, according to producers, to convey "the flavor of the projected locale" in each show. It does not always come across as being different from any other flavor, but more about that later.

CHAPTER THREE

Producers and Writers

IN television, the producers and writers are creative kings. What they say is law, and that law is transmitted on the airwaves into millions of homes (sometimes sixty or seventy million) per night. A popular variety or adventure show or a lovable sitcom will invariably draw a larger audience than an address by a president of the United States, unless the president happens to be announcing his resignation.

Who are these powerful producers and writers, and where do they come from?

What follows is an impressionistic portrait of those producers and writers I have interviewed and worked with.

With a small number of exceptions, they are all white males. They are almost never younger than 35. They are almost never second-generation Californians. A distinct majority, especially of the writers of situation comedies, is Jewish. However, there are many Protestants and Catholics as well, especially among writers of adventure shows.

A writer-producer who is working steadily is well off financially. The pay for producing a TV show compares favorably with the pay for almost any other occupation. By and large, writers and producers lead quiet lives. There is not even a hint of the Sodom-and-Gomorrah type of life that is often associated with the Hollywood of old, and might appropriately be identified with the record business of today. Almost all writers and producers are married and have children, to whom they report faithfully at the end of the day. Almost all live in the western region of Los Angeles, which means Beverly Hills, Holmby Hills, Bel Air, Brentwood, Malibu, or Santa Monica. A large number come from New York City. Only one that I know of comes from what might be thought of as a socially elegant background, although several come from upper-middle-class backgrounds, and none come from poverty.

None that I met had an extensive education, although most were college-educated, even if short of a degree. Few had attended a famous or academically prestigious college or graduate school, although this is certainly a subjective judgment. (In Los Angeles, the University of Southern California might be considered a prestigious school, while in Cambridge that would be considered a joke.)

All of them were happy that they were making as much money as they were, but they all also believed that they should be making more. Even producers making $10,000 a week (and they are not rare) referred to people who were earning more, supposedly from the sweat of the $10,000-a-week slaves. All, including the most highly paid, were acutely conscious of the fact that real wealth in America came from manufacturing or banking or something they were not doing. (When I asked a producer earning more than $250,000 a year how to make money in Hollywood, he said, "Have a father who manufactures shoes.") All of them, even those with millions of dollars, believed themselves to be part of a working class distinctly at odds with the exploiting classes—who, if the subject came up, were identified as the Rockefellers and multinational corporations. For an obscure reason, the name of Nixon was also thrown in frequently.

Almost all were superficially well-informed on matters of current interest and knew the names and claims to fame of those in the news. However, few followed any current issues in depth.

Most were extremely cheerful by the standards of other people with whom I have worked. (I have worked for many governmental and academic bureaucracies, as well as for newspapers, law firms, and magazines.) Comedy writers are constantly making jokes, as one might expect, and as far as I could tell they have an optimistic attitude about everything they do. There was always superb rapport between the producers and writers—who might be thought of as the bosses—and the secretaries and messengers. Some, especially the top people at Tandem/TAT (where I spent a lot of time), had truly extraordinary social skills, in terms of diplomacy, tact, and friendly interchange—skills of a higher order than any I have ever encountered. All thought of themselves as politically "progressive," a term that I have rarely heard elsewhere but that was quite popular among those I interviewed and knew as colleagues.

Although this is a highly subjective conclusion, I believe that some of the people I interviewed did not consider themselves as visual or literary artists but rather saw themselves as craftsmen or fabricators of a highly salable commodity. This was partly an appealing lack of affectation, but it was also a method of rationalizing the small amount of creative control that any one person ever has over the finished product on a TV show.

Most, however, explicitly thought of themselves as artists. No matter how transitory their product, writers and producers generally saw themselves in a league with painters, sculptors, and novelists. All recognized the temporality of their artistry—"like painting on Kleenex," one said—but still, they were artists just the same in their own eyes. (And in mine.)

Their personalities and the way they relate to the world of 1978 is a fascinating subject, and one that will come up later. It has, in my opinion, a powerful bearing on the way TV shows turn out.

CHAPTER FOUR

Businessmen on Television

IN the summer of 1977, a play entitled *The Quadrangle* was presented at a small theatre in Beverly Hills. The author of the play was Arthur Ross, writer of over one hundred teleplays and over twenty screenplays. The plot was about relations between psychiatrists and their patients and about the relation of predators to their prey. A fundamental theme, expressed in several different ways, was that the world is run by hardened, beastly people without consciences who torture and kill those weaker than they. In America, the play said, those stronger, more vicious people take the form of big businessmen. To further demonstrate the point, *The Quadrangle* had as a crucial plot element a giant multinational company's takeover of the Mafia, which was to be used as a muscle arm for the company. The small audience (which filled the small theatre) roared with approval at those sentiments.

Indeed, it would have been foolish to expect anything else, because one of the clearest messages of television is that businessmen are bad, evil people, and that big businessmen are the worst of all. This concept is shared by a distinct majority of the writers and producers I spoke with. Since this attitude is so interesting and so clear, it bears being the first social and cultural message and attitude to be examined.

In TV comedies, businessmen play several different roles, all highly unflattering. Often they are con men. Appearing unannounced, they promise the money-starved regular characters a way out of their poverty. Then, having bilked our loveable favorites, they disappear without a trace. Sometimes they simply appear as pompous fools, bullying and overbearing our regulars until a devastating joke blows them off the set. Some examples follow.

On a recent episode of "Good Times," a banker approached J. J., the teenage son in the poverty-stricken black family, and asked him to paint a mural for a new bank branch. After J. J. had painted it, putting his heart, soul, and hopes into it, the banker refused to pay him.

On "The Mary Tyler Moore Show," in the valedictory episode, a hard-headed businessman was brought in to salvage the ratings of WJM, the fictional station where the most appealing human beings on earth worked and played. He fired Mary and all her friends. In an earlier episode, a fast-talking businessman convinced Ted Baxter, the newscaster on the station, to back a "famous broadcasters' school." Ted, a buffoon, was broken-hearted when the con man fled with the students' money, leaving Ted to make up the loss.

On "Laverne & Shirley," a wealthy, fat entrepreneur tried to make Laverne a star. But he told her that she would have to stop hanging around with her soulmate, Shirley. Otherwise, the rich man of business said, Laverne would simply remain a yokel forever.

On "Maude," Maude's harassed husband Walter went bankrupt in the retail home appliance business. When he announced his loss to his fellow businessmen, they threw rotten eggs and vegetables at him at a Chamber of Commerce dinner. In another episode, Maude sought a donation for her campaign for office from a wealthy businessman, who demanded that she change her position on a number of issues and then deprived her of the contribution.

On the short-lived "All's Fair," a businessman with extremely right-wing ideas was revealed to be a hypocritical sex fiend.

And on it goes. The most succinct summary of the way businessmen are shown in TV comedies came from a producer at a successful comedy production company. A writer approached him with an idea: How about a comedy with businessmen who were good guys? The producer's answer was, "Impossible."

But businessmen are positively glorified on sitcoms compared to their appearance in adventure shows. There, they are almost always criminals in disguise—and murderers more likely than not. Behind the three-piece pinstripe suit, the inevitable badge of crime, lurks the heart of a Bluebeard. The depths of depravity of these fictional characters is truly impressive.

One of my favorite examples appeared on the now-defunct "Harry O," about an eccentric private eye, Harry Orwell. A girl had been murdered. Among the suspects were her boyfriend, a junkie, a hired killer, and her employer, who owned an architectural business. As it happened, the killer was the businessman.

On a show aired in the summer of 1977, "Baretta," a teenage girl was killed by an overdose of heroin. After an excursion through New York's nether world, the detective, Tony Baretta, found that the man who had supplied the heroin was not a pimp—not a murdering dope dealer—but a banker who, behind the scenes, was the kingpin of a dope empire.

On a recent "Hawaii-Five-O" episode, a rotund nursing home operator was compelling his elderly wards to swindle the government of millions of dollars. When one of the patients balked, he was rubbed out by the jolly nursing home entrepreneur.

On a recent "Starsky and Hutch," an art collector and dealer used his connections and position to import and sell heroin.

Not even the smallest of businessmen is exempt from the mark of Cain. In a recent episode of "Kojak," a local candy store owner in New York was, in reality, fencing stolen goods and giving the teenage suppliers heroin. In an extremely similar episode, Kojak discovered that a businessman and a dentist who sponsored a little league team forced the youngsters on the team to steal for their fencing operation.

On almost every episode of "Columbo," a rich businessman has killed someone and seeks to bully Columbo into leaving him alone because of his high status. (Needless to say, he never succeeds.)

The well-dressed businessman who pays for his kids' orthodontia by selling heroin to teenagers and the manufacturer who has murdered his go-go dancer girlfriend are staples of TV adventure shows. Of course, there are many staple plots, and even a few original ones, so that the evil businessman does not dominate the airwaves. However, the murderous, duplicitous, cynical businessman is about the only kind of businessman there is on TV adventure shows, just as the cunning, trickster businessman shares the stage with the pompous buffoon businessman in situation comedies.

If one grants that businessmen are not held in high esteem by the population generally—as one must—television's treatment is still harsh. In fact, few businessmen in three-piece suits commit violent crimes, and even a nodding acquaintance with the drug trade is sufficient to show that drug dealers do not often wear three-piece suits or work as bankers or stock brokers during the day.

What, then, is the point of reference for all the fictional businessmen who kill go-go dancers and rob the poor? Among other possible sources is the feeling of TV writers and producers towards businessmen—a feeling of animosity.

To start with a relatively sanguine comment, a major adventure-show producer who asked for anonymity said that "business controls our lives far more than we'll ever know."

Still in the vein of moderation, Gary Marshal, the fabulously successful producer of "Laverne and Shirley" and "Happy Days," sees big business behind the government. "When the government says something, I'm never sure whether the government is telling the truth, or whether it's big business talking." If big business is talking, Marshal does not generally believe them. "They're always hyping people," he says.

One of the most interesting comments on businessmen came from Jerry Thorpe, the former producer of "Harry O" and a man with years of credentials in TV production, starting as far back as "Playhouse 90". Thorpe sees businessmen as "ambitious, driven, and self-destructive." Businessmen, as Thorpe sees them, are so repressed that they have powerful violence locked up within them. Thorpe adds that the idea of businessmen as killers is pitched to him by writers so often that he has to restrain them.

Stanley Kramer, a world-famous producer of both movies and TV shows, sees business as "part of a very great power structure which wields enormous power over the people."

Meta Rosenberg, producer of "The Rockford Files," sees businessmen themselves as individuals. But she also sees them as part of a "dangerous concentration of power."

Jim Brooks, one of the most gifted writers in television and the producer of "The Mary Tyler Moore Show," has more specific comments on businessmen: "They're all sons of bitches. They're all cannibals. I think of them as eating their own, like in the GE price-fixing scandal. They commit fraud when they say they are interested in anything but profit. They distrust people who are brilliant."

Allen Burns, partner of Brooks and also a brilliant writer and a producer of "The Mary Tyler Moore Show," agrees that he is "pretty unsympathetic toward businessmen." He distrusts and dislikes big business because of its "bigness." He believes that large companies have private armies, which frightens him.

Bob Schiller, a classy name in TV comedy production who wrote for Red Skelton and for Lucille Ball (for thirteen years) and also wrote and produced "Maude" and the ill-starred "All's Fair," said of businessmen, "I don't judge. I think there are good lepers and bad lepers. By and large, because of the structure of our laws, I think that most business is amoral." Schiller cites as examples the "constant outcroppings of bribery, extortion, at-

tempts to bend laws to their own use, interlocking direc-
torates, and so forth."

While the negative view of businessmen was predominant, it was not completely unanimous. Indeed, a few of
the comments were highly favorable. Mort Lachman, a
producer-writer with long experience writing for Bob
Hope and other major comedians and now in charge of
"All In The Family," notes that business is "in some ways
terrifically inventive and effective." He is fond of one
company in particular: "IBM has led the way." He believes that competition is the essence of making business
act decently. But even Lachman, whose views were unusually favorable, believes that all too often business be-
haves the way it did in *Network,* a popular movie of 1976
and 1977 whose central theme was that the world is run
by huge businesses with the sole aim of expansion and
profit.

An answer on business and businessmen which con-
tained an unusual amount of social criticism as well as
predictive content came from Douglas Benton, who has
written or produced for "Police Woman," "Columbo,"
"Ironside," "The Name of the Game," and many others.
"Leftists have made 'big business' the 'heavy,' " he said,
"the culprit for what's wrong with everything. People on
the right, the capitalists, are saying it's the answer because it's the only way creative enterprise can flourish."
(Benton, like many others, used "business" and "free
enterprise" or "market economy" synonymously.) "It's
economic democracy at work. It's the strong smart people who get all the money and the weak dumb people
who suffer. That's economic democracy? It's like what
Winston Churchill said about democracy, that it's one of

the worst systems ever put together. Very little can be said about it that's good or worthwhile. The only thing that can be said about it is that it's better than anything else.

"Big business is not very efficient. It tends to rob people of creativity. It tends to stultify them. . . . The big corporations like GM and IBM are dinosaurs. They will die out after my lifetime. We are inevitably moving toward socialism. It's been happening ever since the democracy was set up. Ultimately it will come to socialism, because it's the only governmental organization which attempts to take care of the dumb and the weak and the helpless. The free enterprise system is set up to reward your energy."

Perhaps the most unusually detailed and sympathetic view of businessmen came from Charlie Hauck, producer of "Maude." Hauck has an unusual background for a TV producer. He was a producer of a children's TV show on the Public Broadcasting Service, and before that he wrote for *Business Week.* His response to a question about his feelings towards big business is worth quoting at length.

Hauck believes he is "more sympathetic to business than are most people in TV . . . more sympathetic than I should be." He also believes he is more privy to its operations than are most people in television because of his work at *Business Week.* "I met very few executives I didn't like or respect," Hauck says, "even when I was at odds with them. Executives in any given corporation tend to collectively make mistakes that they don't view as mistakes. They are like small towns in that respect. They are narrow-minded. They sincerely don't understand why welfare mothers are picketing the lobby of their bank if they don't distribute food stamps.

"The bank and the mothers see themselves differently. The bank wants to maximize profits. The welfare mothers want the bank to do something for the community. The mothers don't put themselves in the position of the bankers and no one expects them to. The bankers don't put themselves in the position of the mothers, but everyone expects them to."

(Another positive view of businessmen came from David Begelman, then president of Columbia Pictures, which includes Columbia Pictures Television. Interestingly enough, I interviewed Begelman in the erroneous belief that he was a former writer and producer. Instead, as I should have known, he is a former lawyer and talent agent. At that time, he was a businessman and head of a large corporation. His views were not only positive but enthusiastic. Begelman saw businessmen as uncommonly intelligent, hardworking, honest, socially committed, patriotic, and devoted to their families.)

Despite the views of Lachman, Benton, and Hauck, however, the predominant view of businessmen is extremely negative, and the conclusion one is left with was well, if scatalogically, summarized by a writer who said that when he thought of businessmen running the country, he got a "clong," which he described as a rush of fecal matter to the heart.

It is important to realize that people who have reached the stage of being writers for or producers of TV shows are similar to businessmen in a number of outward respects. For one thing, they are all in business, trying to produce a product or service and sell it for more than it cost to make it. Also, both groups share in the success of their enterprise by making more money (in the case of producers, far more) if the product is successful than if it is not. And both groups share the uncertainties of life in a highly competitive world.

A dimension of the TV writers' image of business, and of big business in particular, is the writers' insistence that it is closely connected with the Mafia. That concept was entirely new to me. It first surfaced spontaneously at an interview. When I included a question about the link between business and the Mafia as part of my questionnaire, and even when I specifically mentioned businesses on the scale of U.S. Steel, I found near unanimity on the answer.

A producer who had worked for many years on adventure shows set all over the country (and recently on two shows set in the Depression in different locales) laid out the matter most baldly: "If you don't believe that the Mafia is running big business, you must be blind."

The late Bruce Geller, a writer and executive producer on "Mission Impossible," "Mannix," "Have Gun Will Travel," and "Bronk," among many others, and then an executive in charge of production at Twentieth Century Fox, got down to cases:

"Of course the two are connected. It's a very shady area. Organized crime has massive amounts of money that is put in extremely legitimate enterprises." Geller pointed out that, in his opinion, many parts of show business are financed by underworld money. "It's understandable in my business where financing is difficult. . . . In any circumstance people tend to take money where they can find it."

Gary Marshal saw the connection plainly. "There's definitely a link between big business and organized crime. There has to be a link to make big business work."

Bob Schiller gave the most popular answer to the question about big business and the Mafia when he said that he saw a link not only between big business and the Mafia but also between government and the Mafia, and between labor and the Mafia.

Again, however, there was less than total unanimity about the situation. Mort Lachman, for one, saw a link but said it was nothing to feel paranoid about. Several people who preferred to remain anonymous simply could not be made to respond to the question as it was asked. They read it as, "Do you personally receive money from the Mafia?" and all denied receiving any.

Not everyone saw the Mafia in bed with IBM and William Blinn, one of the biggest guns in TV writing and author of one or more episodes of "Roots," "Starsky and Hutch," "The New Land," "The Rookies," "Bonanza," and "The Interns," gave a unique and unequivocal answer: "There is a conscious, deliberate un-relationship [sic] between big business and organized crime. They tend to leave each other alone. It's mutually understood that they have their own territory. By not competing, they actually help each other. They allow each other to thrive in their separate fields." But the comment of Stanley Kramer that "the Mafia is part of the entire corporate entity now" is far more representative than Blinn's.

To some extent, the allegation that the Mafia is linked with business explains why businessmen are shown to be such bad people on television. If the businessman is really a Mafioso, then we could hardly expect him to be anything but a bad man. Even if the businessman is a silent partner of the Mafia, he is still a different person from Horatio Alger's businessman. But that leads to another question. Why is there such widespread belief in the link between the Mafia and the business world? The belief itself is a phenomenon I had never encountered before.

Part of the answer may be that it is true—the Mafia might be an integral part of the corporate structure. It may be that TV writers have simply discovered something I did not know. Certainly they have often led fuller lives than I have where business is concerned. But a larger part of the reason why so many people think the Mafia is linked to business comes, in my opinion, from the prevailing conspiracy theory of history. In Hollywood, almost nothing is explained except on the basis of conspiracies and cabals. It is here, for example, that serious, intelligent people believe that the world is run by a consortium of former Nazis and executives of multinational corporations.

Why Hollywood should be wedded to the conspiracy explanation of human events is beyond my knowing for certain. It probably has something to do with the unpredictability and randomness of human life in Hollywood, especially in terms of success and failure. It is difficult for people to come to grips with the randomness of events, and rather than do so, they often invent complex reasons for phenomena. Perhaps my reasoning in itself is an example of the prevalence of conspiracy explanations. At any rate, for some reason, people who write for television believe that there is a definite link between the Mafia and business, especially big business.

A further explanation of the animosity TV writers feel toward businessmen is that TV writers know something about business. The writer aiming to make a great deal of money in Hollywood is quite different from most intellectuals or academic writers. The latter usually deal with business and businessmen as abstractions, either good or bad. If they deal with real businessmen besides the ones who fix their cars, those businessmen tend to be elder-statesmen types or public relations men. Academics and editorial writers do not conduct business with business-men except for the occasional purchase of a speech or an article.

The Hollywood TV writer, on the other hand, is actu-ally in a business, selling his labor to brutally callous businessmen. One actually has to go through the experi-ence of writing for money in Hollywood or anywhere else to realize just how unpleasant it is. Most of the pain comes from dealings with business people, such as agents or business affairs officers of production companies and net-works. The number of calamities that can and do happen can hardly be believed unless they are experienced. The TV writer is not an honored guest at a meeting of busi-nessmen at the Greenbriar. He is actually down there in the pit with the clawing agents and businessmen, and he often has reason to feel that he has been shortchanged, to say the least. It was fascinating to notice that those who were the most positive toward businessmen were those whose experiences with them were not adversary but rather collegial or reportorial. On the other hand, those who had been writers all their lives usually felt the most anger toward businessmen, and with good reason.

There are yet other explanations for why the business-man comes off so badly in Hollywood. The key one is that businessmen, especially big businessmen, are per-ceived as coming from a different class from that of the TV writers and producers—and an adversary one at that. Although not one producer or writer said so for the record, a number of writers with whom I became familiar spoke of businessmen from AT&T or IBM in terms that contrasted their Gentile, Ivy League backgrounds with the more ethnic, "school-of-hard-knocks" backgrounds of the TV writers.

There was a distinct feeling that, despite the high pay and the access to powerful media that TV writers and producers enjoy, they are still part of a despised underclass, oppressed psychologically and (potentially) physically by an Aryan ruling class of businessmen and others. This feeling was by no means confined to Jews.

The belief in a ruling class of white, East Coast Protestants meeting occasionally in corporate board rooms to give its orders to whoever happens to be elected to office is so strong that no amount of argument to the contrary makes a dent. And hostility to that real or imagined class is just as strong.

But whatever the reasons for the situation, the net result of it is that on prime-time TV shows, businessmen and business are despised. And that portrayal fits well with the general, although not unanimous, vision of businessmen and business in the community of Hollywood TV writers.

CHAPTER FIVE

Crime on Television

🙥🙥🙥 **N**OTHING is more certain
on television than crime. Indeed, crime provides the single most recurrent theme on prime-time television. While the balance between crime shows and situation comedies fluctuates (lately it has been weighted toward situation comedies), there are a variety of motive concepts on sitcoms, while adventure shows always involve a crime.

And when those crimes occur, they are always violent. There may be a lot of income tax evasion and embezzlement in real life, but on a TV show it's murder, rape, armed robbery, and kidnapping that count. Parents, teachers, and other interest groups have declaimed against the rising tide of violence on television, and even though that tide is slowly receding, the basic point is well taken. There is an amazing amount of killing, raping, robbing, and kidnapping on prime-time television by almost any standard, except perhaps in comparison with real life and death in a big American city.

But the crime shows are clearly not showing us life as it really is where crime is concerned. The main reason for the gap between TV crime and real-life crime is the nature of the criminal. There are also problems with the nature of the victim and the nature of the crime.

In real-life murders, rapes, and so forth, both victims

and perpetrators are usually poor, minority-group people, apparently acting on sudden impulses of rage and anger. Robberies and muggings also are usually perpetrated by young minority-group males, although there is some evidence that there is a great deal of caclulation in those crimes. But there, too, the victim is often another ghetto dweller.

On television, things could hardly be more different. The typical TV murder involves a well-to-do white person killing another well-to-do white person. The crimes almost always are premeditated, with careful planning taking place weeks or even months before the event. The criminal is a comfortable middle-class or upper-middle-class person, even if not a businessman. If minority group teenagers are involved at all, they either are cat's-paws of the well-to-do or are being made the fall guys for crimes they did not commit.

A typical example, distinguished only by the ludicrous extent to which it carries the basic theme, occurred recently on "Streets of San Francisco." A beautiful co-ed had been found brutally murdered, right there on the campus. The suspects were a Chicano who was on parole for another violent crime, a student junkie who was having an affair with the wife of a medical professor, and—apparently—no one else. As it happened, the killer was the dead girl's roommate, who was having a lesbian affair with her and murdered her out of jealousy, planting incriminating evidence on others. In fact, women on big city campuses become the victims of violent crimes committed by neighboring ghetto youths with depressing regularity on television, but I have almost never heard of a case quite like the one on "Streets of San Francisco."

If the perpetrators are not well-to-do or middle-class

Caucasians, they are well-to-do or middle-class non-whites. The black pimp, rolling in money and swagger, has recently made his appearance as the heavy, although he too is more often falsely accused than genuinely guilty of anything except flesh-peddling—a far cry, in the TV world of 1977, from a really serious crime.

Occasionally, a mentally-ill white punk will be a criminal, but in that case there is always some interesting quirk in his background that lifts the story out of the realm of real life or facsimile. For instance, on a recent "Starsky and Hutch," a white punk detained and raped a pretty, mentally-retarded teenage girl on an empty school bus. When the girl was coaxed into testifying against the punk, a smart-aleck lawyer got him paroled so that he could go out and terrify the girl again. The punk's motivation, aside from general meanness, was that he owed a loan-shark money and the debt was depressing him. Even in that episode, the real villains were middle-class—the loan shark and the lawyer—though the actual rapist was a punk.

In the thousands of hours I have spent watching adventure shows, I have never seen a major crime committed by a poor, teenage, black, Mexican, or Puerto Rican youth, even though they account for a high percentage of all violent crime. As with the strange treatment of the businessmen, the question that arises is, "Why?" And, again, it is clear that there is at least some explanation to be found in the attitudes of TV writers and producers toward crime and criminals. The overwhelming majority of TV writers is far more concerned with white-collar crime and with organized crime than with street crime. Further, the overwhelming majority of TV writers and producers believes that the blame for violent street crime rests not on the criminal, but on some larger social failure or on the intention of our particular society.

It is instructive to look at the comments.

Stephen Kandel, one of the most prolific and highly regarded writers for television, when asked what the causes of crime were, answered, "Frustration, rage, structural incompetence, social reasons, psychological reasons." When the question was refined to cover only violent crime, Kandel answered, "Are you talking about Dean Rusk? Richard Nixon? Were they violent criminals? They bombed Cambodia and killed two million people." He attributed this particular "crime" to the setting up of a social and governmental structure that "defies accountability."

When asked specifically about violent street crime, Kandel, whose writing credits include pilots and scripts for "Wonder Woman," "Star Trek," "Cannon," "Hawaii-Five-O," "The Bionic Woman," "The Six Million Dollar Man," "Barnaby Jones," "Streets of San Francisco," "Switch," "Mannix," "Mission Impossible," and many, many others, replied that the cause was the lack of opportunity to participate in the desirable social life of the community. "Part of the blame rests with TV for raising people's expectations," Kandel added, launching into a lengthy exemplary story about how summer jobs in New York were given to the children of political cronies instead of to the poor, which incites poor people to violence.

Kandel's proposed solution to the problem of crime harmonized completely with his ideas about the causes of crime. The answer, for Kandel, was "to provide avenues of achievement and employment, and an adjustment between population and employment." He added that the really difficult problem to solve would be white-collar crime, because "the class that makes the laws and enforces them participates in the crime and gets rewarded by the crime."

Stanley Kramer, too, saw society and its misdeeds as the main reason for crime. "Wars generate crime to a greater degree than people realize. Crime comes from wars and repressions and ghettoes." (In a truly startling statement, Kramer then added, "Everything that has to do with our lives is contaminated. The air, the streams, the food—everything is ruined.") Kramer, like Kandel, believed that street crime will be easier to stop than crime in industry or government.

Meta Rosenberg also was more concerned with organized crime than with street crime, which she saw as caused by drugs and "disorientation in the society." Bob Schiller felt the cause of crime was the gap between "the American dream and the American reality." Schiller's partner, Bob Weiskopf, saw the cause of crime as "socio-economic, and I think the 'socio' is dependent on the 'economic.' I think much of it [the cause of crime,] is the economics of our society; poor people, oppressed people. I suspect the bulk of the crimes are committed by people who are poor and oppressed." Weiskopf's solution fits his conception of the cause perfectly: the redistribution of wealth.

Lee Rich, president of Lorimar Productions (a significant factor in TV production) and writer or producer of such TV shows as "Eight Is Enough" and "The Waltons" and TV films such as *Sybil, Helter-Skelter,* and others, sees similar causes of crime. "Frustration and what we in America have done to racial and economic minorities.

People see every day in newspapers and TV evidence of those who have and those who have not. They look at this and they think, 'Why shouldn't I have it?' I should hope that they would reach those goals in an appropriate manner, but very often, the frustration leads them to seek their goals through crime." Apparently unaware of facts to the contrary, Rich asserted that "in the world we have built there is almost no middle class any more. There is a lower class and a medium-to-upper class. That has helped to incur crime."

A woman producer of adventure shows who wished to be nameless gave a similar answer about the causes of crime: "Poverty, lack of education, drugs."

Thad Mumford, a story editor on "Maude," had a lengthy but close to paradigmatic explanation of the situation. "The environment causes it," he said flatly (and then added that perhaps there was also some validity to the chromosome theory of violent behavior). Mumford noted that a young person in Harlem could easily have the motivation to turn to crime. "He sees the incongruity of life. He sees the white suburbanites coming through Harlem on the trains." Mumford could understand why a poor child seeing white commuters would turn to crime. "It makes sense to me," Mumford said. "I hope they don't do anything bad to me, but I understand it." In speaking about a possible solution for the crime problem, Mumford was deeply pessimistic. Like most of his colleagues, he saw the problem and the solution originating at the top of society. "If there is a solution," Mumford said, "it involves a complete scraping away of the ghettoes." By this, he meant not the liquidation of the people in the ghettoes, but rather the creation of far better living areas for them. "There would have to be a rethinking of white supremacy. The need to elevate whites above all others would have to go.

"All the strides that have been made so far are just token gestures," Mumford said. He then went into a lengthy discussion of how society really operates, in his opinion, and the impossibility of changing it. "The people who have the money have always had it," he said. To that fact he attributed many of the flaws in society. "The people with money are invisible. They are white WASPs." He gave an example of the hopelessness of the situation. "There is no way a kid from Harlem can attain a position at Chase Manhattan. To attain real decision-making power is impossible for people without the right background." Then Mumford wondered, "Where do the Harold Geneens come from? They seem to exist by themselves. They are so far removed from society that they don't know what people think about." The existence of what Mumford believed to be the remote white power elite was, to Mumford, the key reason for crime in America.

Leonard Goldberg, a partner in today's most successful producer of adventure shows, Spelling-Goldberg, Inc., sees social causes in the crime in real life as well as on television. "People commit crimes because they are frustrated and angry, and because of the accessibility of weapons. There is a decay of morality. Laws are disregarded. There is no respect for contracts between individuals. . . . Crime begins with unemployment. A man who can't get a job is an angry man."

The above explanations for the causes of violent crime are far and away the modal explanations of the TV writer.

There is, however, a current of opinion that places responsibility for crime on the criminal, not on the society. Gary Marshal was the only producer or writer to subscribe to the recently popularized theory that criminals commit crimes out of a calculation that it is economically worthwhile to do so. While Marshal thought that the main reason people commit crimes is to "feel special," he also thinks that "poor people do it to get money. It's easier to commit a crime than to work hard and become a success."

Charlie Hauck, producer of "Maude," went even further in ascribing responsibility for crimes to criminals. "The basic cause of crime," Hauck said, "is that people don't think they have to play by the rules. The environment does not dictate that attitude. Environment persuades people with a penchant for crime to either follow that penchant or not.

"Where there's more poverty, there's more crime. Yet not everyone who lives in poverty commits crimes. Tendency to commit crime predates environment. Family conditions and family attitudes determine this attitude."

Hauck has a similarly personal idea of how to stop crime. "There must be rules. There must be consequences for breaking the rules. There must be certainty about the consequences. We must be enlightened about the consequences, but consequences should not be less. We must have saner people having children. Most of us don't know how to raise children. The main thing wrong is not letting children accept all the responsibility they can as early as they can."

Bruce Geller saw racial motives and causes in some crime. "I'm not convinced that social programs are effective," he said. "I don't see that much has happened from the outpourings of funds and good will. . . . My father was a judge and dealt with crime daily. This isn't a racial slur, but most of the people who came in front of him were black, Puerto Rican, and not from the first generation but from the second generation."

Geller also sees cities as places where bad people can get bad ideas. "I'm an anthropologist by background, and I would call it [the city] a cultural sink. There's a great deal of volition in crime, of pleasure, of group inactivity; it becomes a system of life. It's also a hideous necessity of poverty," Geller added, following a popular line of thought. Then he said, "Crime is plain hostility, too, and racial conflict."

Douglas Benton saw crime as being caused primarily by poverty but also largely by a person's choice to be a criminal, a view similar to Hauck's. "There are some very nice people, whom you would like to have to your house for dinner, who are crooks. They can't help themselves. Given a choice between being dull and straight or interesting and crooked, they'll choose to be crooks. . . . We are just on the frontier of trying to discover what goes on in the criminal mind. Crime is a psychological cancer. Once it starts, you can't get rid of it."

But any explanations of crime that are not rooted in a condemnation of society and of the social system are minority views in this group, and thereby hangs a possibility of explaining why television treats crime as it does.

The Hollywood TV producer sees crime as being rooted in the middle class or upper middle class. He sees the classes that, to his mind, control society as controlling the causes of crime. Although the black 15-year-old may actually wield the gun, it is the well-heeled suburbanite who forces him not to go to medical school and instead to become a vicious killer. By a process of short-cutting the actual and moving directly into the theoretical, the TV producer can simply make the criminal the well-heeled suburbanite. The minority group youths, seen as utterly innocent and victimized by all of this social incompetence, are relieved of any responsibility on TV shows simply by not being shown doing anything bad.

While that may be the main reason for the cast of TV villains being what it is, there are other reasons as well. Some producers said that there was more drama in an adventure show if the criminal was socially more elevated than a street kid. Such a "twist" makes the plot more interesting than if youth gangs were shown to be responsible for crimes time after time. That argument is advanced seriously, even though the real twist would be if a ghetto youth were shown to have committed the crime after suspicion had fallen on the vicar of the local Episcopal church. A twist, one would think, is something that happens less often than the mode.

Yet another reason for crime's taking place in the never-never land of antiseptic affluence is that interest-group pressure has been brought to bear. David Begelman, ex-president of Columbia Pictures, states flatly that all criminals on television are white because of pressure from lobbyists from various ethnic minorities. The problem with that explanation is that lobbyists usually respond to an *existing* situation. NAACP lobbyists, for instance, might claim that television was showing too many blacks as killers and protest. However, there never has been a time when minority group members were shown as criminals on television, so there would have been nothing to lobby against and no racial defamation to eliminate.

In any event, no matter what other facts or theories appear, two propositions stand out. First, TV shows almost never show crime or criminals as they are. Second, TV writers and producers do not hold criminals responsible for crime but rather place the blame on society.

CHAPTER SIX

Police on Television

☙☙☙ **I**N REAL LIFE, so the saying goes, you can never find a policeman when you need one. But in the world of television, there are policemen everywhere. Every adventure show, whether it stars policemen in uniform, plainclothesmen, private detectives, or even beautiful women posing as police agents, has police. Except for criminals, no other single occupational group gets as much air time as police.

Unlike the fairly clear and uniform way in which businessmen are treated negatively and criminals are treated forgivingly, the treatment of police on television is far from straightforward or consistent. Television's attitude toward the men in blue (or in T-shirts or whatever they may be wearing) is a mixture of love and hate, admiration and scorn. But there is a deep well of affection.

On a show like "Kojak," where the hero, Theo Kojak, is a policeman, the portraits of him and his closest associates are unrelievedly flattering. On the other hand, his superiors far up the line may be bumbling and pretentious. On "Baretta," the tough plainclothes detective hardly ever does anything wrong. Yet his colleagues in other departments, his superiors, or his inferiors may screw up constantly.

"Charlie's Angels" shows a winsome detective trio

who can usually get help from the police, but whom the police are often fighting. "Police Story" tells of the heroism of policemen, but often in the context of other policemen who are cowardly or venal. "Columbo" shows an unorthodox cop who tries to keep his nose clean while following leads that his supervisors deny exist. "Hawaii-Five-O" tells about a team of crack policemen who show no human imperfections. "Starsky and Hutch," no saints themselves, are constantly hamstrung by the interference and pusillanimity of their colleagues. Starsky and Hutch themselves often miss clues and make incorrect deductions. In addition, their brutality is frequently startling. On "Streets of San Francisco," the policemen on the beat are frighteningly ineffectual, while the administrators of the police department constantly throw bureaucratic roadblocks in the way of the success-ful completion of an investigation.

In general, while the heroes of cop shows are highly admirable, the other policemen on the scene are no-where near so appealing. There is bravery and coward-ice, brutality and compassion, skill and incompetence. Although TV shows maintain a high degree of clarity in the images of most elements of life, the police picture is muddled indeed at first glance.

Not surprisingly, in interviews with TV writers and writer-producers, a mixed bag of opinions about police appeared. The interviews showed reactions of respect and contempt and affection and fear, in addition to other attitudes that do not appear to have any visible product on television. Feelings about cops are often much more personal and less abstract than feelings about other groups in society, and they were expressed more vividly.

Meta Rosenberg expressed an unusually detailed but

typically personal view of the police. Rosenberg believed that the police were in her employ. "They're there to look after me," she said. She noted that the police in Beverly Hills are especially polite, as she expects them to be. She told a story of a Beverly Hills policeman who stopped her when she was jaywalking. The policeman instructed her to go down to a corner and cross the street again. "I told him that he was treating me like a child and I would not stand for it," she said. "I told him to either give me a ticket or leave. I really yelled at him," she recalled, "and he just got in his car and drove away."

Rosenberg noted that usually the Beverly Hills police are better even than that, in that they are more polite. Her feelings about the way other people might look at the police and about police other than the ones in Beverly Hills were sharply different. She believed that if she lived in the ghetto, she might feel very differently. Black people and young people are "hassled" by the police, she believed.

She also believed that the Los Angeles police were far better than the police in other cities, where, she felt, they are owned by the Mafia, treat people badly, and even sell drugs. Despite her high praise for the Los Angeles police department, she spoke angrily about former Los Angeles police chief Ed Davis, whom she called ". . . an asshole, a reactionary son of a bitch." That attitude was shared by some and sharply controverted by others, as we will see.

Stephen Kandel said flatly that he believes the police are ineffective. He saw the police as failing at their three major functions: solving crimes, regulating social behavior, and preventing crimes. Kandel believed the police were particularly ineffective at dealing with white-collar crime. In addition, he said, they enforced the law in a

highly biased way, without examining the statutory basis
of the crime. "Symbolically, the police are a disaster,"
Kandel added. "They are a paranoid in-group. They are
no longer the friendly father figures on the beat."

Kandel, like Rosenberg, expressed highly negative
feelings about the Los Angeles police chief, whom he
thought tried harder to maintain certain social attitudes
than to prevent crime. "Davis won't prosecute for wife
beating or child abuse," Kandel said, "but he does inter-
vene in prostitution and political deviation." This priority,
Kandel believed, was wrong.

The concern over policemen's being or becoming a
"paranoid in-group" was expressed by several different
writers in different ways. William Blinn said, "Being a cop
is the worst job in the world. It breeds an insular, dangerous mental attitude. We insulate cops. They cluster
together in little tight groups with no contact with the
public. Cops' minds get warped from lack of contact with
the public and too much grouping amongst themselves."

Mort Lachman noted that a policeman's life can make
him more brutal than the criminal. When that happens,
he said, policemen "are interested mainly in making
something like a fraternity." Like many others interviewed, Lachman referred to a novel by Joseph Wam-
baugh called *The Choirboys,* which dealt with brutalized
policemen who become cliquish and calloused. Like others, Lachman blamed not the police themselves, but
rather their "terrifying" work.

Several writers said that policemen were dramatically
underpaid and ill-treated. Lee Rich said that "they're underpaid, work hard—it's a terrible job. We have a penchant in this country for underpaying very important jobs,
people who serve and protect the public, like policemen

and school teachers. It's the most thankless job in the world. Because of this it attracts corruption, just to get even. If schoolteachers had the opportunity to become corrupt they would, because they're so underpaid." Similar sentiments about ill-treatment and inadequate pay were expressed by at least a dozen other writers and producers.

While many sympathized with the police in several areas, few were as unabashedly positive as David Begelman. He saw the police as "capable and efficient." He said, "They have the opportunity to be corrupt, but the percentage of corruption is small compared to [what it is in] the private sector. The temptation for brutality is not indulged." Begelman singled out the Beverly Hills police for special commendation. He also had high praise for Chief Ed Davis of Los Angeles. "He's a very tough cop. He imposes stringent standards on the police, and that's good."

Even Begelman's encomium paled before Douglas Benton's, which is worth quoting at length. "Who else do you know who would risk his life to return your automobile or to stop a domestic quarrel time after time for $800 a month? It takes a special kind of person to do that. . . . They're doing their job. They're dedicated. They're doing their job remarkably well considering the limitations they have to work in."

Benton then explained in detail why the police spend time on "victimless" crimes like the use of marijuana or prostitution. "According to their experience, once you find prostitution it won't be long before you find dope and then murder. You start with a joint and end up with killings. That's the policeman's attitude toward innocent dope smokers. It's a preventive as far as they're concerned."

In sum, a confused picture of police emerged. Police were considered effective and inept, corrupt and honest, brutalized and compassionate (one producer had tears in his eyes while talking about the sensitivity of cops to derelicts), often by the same person. However, there was an almost unanimous feeling of being able to relate personally to the police, as well as a powerful note of sympathy. Like the belief that criminals act criminally because of a social flaw, the belief that police do not succeed because society mistreats them is almost universally held.

This confusion, anger, and sympathy are reflected clearly in TV fare. There is a counterpart for almost every kind of policeman or police problem that the writers mentioned. The corrupt cop, the heroic cop, the underpaid cop (always with a wife who wants more money), the burnt-out case cop—all these make their appearance regularly on television.

One TV counterpart does not appear undisguised, though—the brutalized, brutal cop. I cannot recall any shows in which a main character was a cop who was seen by the other cops or by any authority figure as overly brutal. Starsky and Hutch come closest, but even their brutality is upheld as good, a shortcut through procedural briar patches. Similarly, only one show, "Police Story," occasionally presents policemen as part of a "paranoid in-group."

Where are the artifacts of the thoughts so powerfully expressed by the producers and writers? In disguise. The TV cops and detectives are, in reality, incredibly brutal by any standard except that of their fellow cops on television, a comparison that tends to blur objectivity. The number of people that a Tony Baretta or a Starsky or a Kojak throws up against a wall and threatens with bodily harm or death becomes startling when added up over a season. Compared with the lives of real human beings, especially the real human beings who write for television, the lives of TV policemen are astonishingly rough. Moreover, TV cops are not fazed at all by the brutality of their lives, a sign that they have been brutalized. Again, this only appears when TV policemen are taken out of the context of television and compared with real people. It is then that the harshness of police life on television appears.

Similarly, in terms of cliques, one tends to forget when watching "Hawaii-Five-O" week in and week out that the policemen associate only with each other. The same is true on all other cop shows. Police are shown with other police, criminals, suspects, and informers, and that is all. There are no next-door neighbors who are firemen or accountants. All police shows present policemen as being highly cliquish, although this only appears when the shows are compared—not with each other—but with life.

Cops, then, are seen in a confused, angry, but basically highly sympathetic way by TV writers and producers as a group—(although individual writers' views are more uniform). With slight modifications to allow for heroes and villains as necessary for drama, that is how they are shown on television.

CHAPTER SEVEN

The Military on Television

Ｗ HILE we are on the subject of a uniformed service, it would be sensible to talk about the largest uniformed service—the American military. On television, the military is shown regularly in a few shows—"M.A.S.H.," "The Bionic Woman," "The Six Million Dollar Man" (usually in plain clothes), and occasionally on others. Movies made especially for television also have occasional military stories, but they are becoming less and less frequent. A show that began in the 1976–1977 season, "Baa-Baa Black Sheep," dealt with Marine pilots in the Pacific during World War II.

When one views shows that deal with the military, a number of different viewpoints pop out from the TV screen, most of them quite negative. The crux of the popular "M.A.S.H." is that the Army is constantly trying to get as many people killed as possible, burn down as many villages as possible, separate loved ones as often as possible, and generally stand in the way of warm and natural human development. Opposing the Army is a group of civilian doctors and orderlies who have been drafted for service in the Korean War. These draftees are able, by sheer imagination and cunning, to fool the Army every time and to assert the forces of warmth and compassion where they would not otherwise exist. The Army on

"M.A.S.H." is sometimes shown running amok, bombing civilians from heights far above where life can be seen. More often, though, the Army is represented by stiff, hypocritical officers—enlisted men are never unsympathetic—who issue nonsensical orders and constantly seek to make themselves seem important.

On "The Bionic Woman," the Air Force has put together a remarkable woman, part human, part machine, who fights bad people. Together with the cryptic intelligence service, O.S.I., the military sends Jamie off to dangerous jungles and the lairs of spies to protect America's freedom. On this show, unlike most others, there are bad foreigners—people who hark back to the pre-1960s days when Americans believed that there were really foreign enemies. The military men who send Jamie off on her missions are invariably good and well-intentioned people. With a few exceptions, they are also stiff and pompous. They are like the stuffed shirts of "M.A.S.H." without the malice. Interestingly enough, their lives are rarely in jeopardy, while Jamie is sent off into danger every week.

Similarly, on "The Six Million Dollar Man" Major Steve Austin, part human, part machine, is sent on dangerous missions by the O.S.I., often with military assistance. His O.S.I. colleagues are certainly the most cheerful and human military or even semimilitary people on television. Sometimes *their* lives are even at risk. They too, however, are empire builders, with Steve Austin occasionally facing more danger from bureaucratic infighting—different spy agencies and parts of the Pentagon warring with each other—than from the enemy without.

On "Baa-Baa Black Sheep," supposedly based on the real-life Pacific Theater adventures of "Pappy Boyington," the characters were quite similar to characters on a cop show. There were a few brave men (and women) who actually went out and faced danger. Then there were the military bureaucrats, making all the wrong decisions and always going "by the book" when a more humane approach would have raised morale, improved fighting capabilities, and shortened the war. "Pappy" and his merry men had to seek constantly to outwit the staff bureaucrats in order to get on with winning the war.

The most violently antimilitray point of view I have ever seen on television came from a recent episode of "Kingston: Confidential," a Raymond Burr vehicle about the adventures of a crusading publisher. A huge United States Army base had been infiltrated by the American Action Clan, which looked a lot like the Ku Klux Klan. The AAC killed a renegade member, which set off an investigation. In the course of the inquiry, conducted by Kingston (Burr) we learned that the American Action Clan was an offshoot of a fundamentalist religious sect whose motto was "Brotherhood Through Loyalty." The head of the sect and the Army general commanding the base were diverting weapons for a right-wing uprising. A lot of blond, clean-shaven young men spied on Kingston until he broke up the group and the Klan-sect plans for national cleansing. The "Kingston: Confidential" episode is particularly revealing because it shows a frequently encountered Hollywood attitude—that the United States Army is the same as the Ku Klux Klan is the same as Protestant fundamentalism. On "Fernwood 2 Night," a similar point of view came out when a veteran announced that he belonged to the Francisco Franco post of the Veterans of Foreign Wars.

The net result of all this, if there is one, is that military men, with the exception of the heroes, are at best part of a bureaucratic background noise that sets off the heroes' humanity. At worst, they are identical to the Nazis they defeated. Hardly ever is there any sign of dedication or true devotion to any principles beyond feathering one's nest and covering one's rear flanks, or worse. Certainly there is no mention of the military's serving any crucial function in the maintenance of peace or freedom or the defense of America from foreign enemies, although individual heroes, like the Bionic Man or the Bionic Woman, may have major responsibilities for averting catastrophe. There is no notion that the military as an institution is doing anything particulary important or worthwhile. The contrast with the sympathetic, although confused, portrait of police is extremely sharp on this point.

And when we look at the feelings of producers and writers on this subject, we see an attitude that is nearly parallel to the point of view on the screen. That attitude is rather interesting and unusual, not only in itself, but also in its difference from what I assume to be more common attitudes about the military.

While opinion on the American military is divided in America, at least some sizable portion of the people presumably believes that the military serves an important role. Since more than $100 billion are voted for the military each year, one might assume that there is some need for a large and strong defense force. Further, common sense alone indicates, at least to some, that there is an external threat from the Soviet Union, and that the military plays an important role in deterring that danger. These views may be held by a large number of people, even if not by an overwhelming majority.

Similarly, one might well think of people in the military as having some devotion to patriotism, duty, or other high ideals. Certainly many books and movies indicate that this view is widely held. And I have met people in the military who are there for reasons other than getting three square meals a day. There is, in short, some positive feeling in the land about the military as a crucial institution with some dedicated people in it.

Among TV writers and producers, on the other hand, there is simply no positive feeling whatsoever about the military. Indeed, the opinions of the TV production people I spoke to about the military contrasted more sharply and more uniformly with the feelings of other Americans than did TV people's opinions in any other area. The most favorable TV writer's opinion towards the military in America was the concept of it as a necessary evil. From then on, it was all downhill.

Bob Schiller summed up the feeling well: "Having been in the military, I think it's idiotic for the most part. I detest the total feeling of distrust that exists in the world [and] that is perpetuated by the military in this and other countries. I think the best that can be said about it [the military] is that it is a necessary evil. I just wish it weren't so necessary and I wish it weren't so evil."

The notion that the military creates the problems it is supposed to solve, and that it is responding to imaginary security dangers that it has generated, was widespread. Bob Weiskopf noted succinctly, "I'm against the military anywhere. The military gets everything it wants by scare tactics, and I'm against that."

Often the concept of imaginary danger was linked with

the idea that the American military is constantly seeking to expand at the expense of the citizens' peace of mind. Mort Lachman said, "If you understand that the military is like all branches of the government—it must grow or die—then you understand the military." Lachman added, "Growth for the military occurs only during a war. The military has to have a present danger, whether it's real or not." As an example, Lachman cited Vietnam, which he characterized as "a war over shots that were never fired."

Charlie Hauck saw the military as "a multitude of people who are more concerned with empire building than with the true needs of defense. They have exploited the Cold War mentality."

Some complaints about the military were more highly differentiated. Stephen Kandel had a detailed indictment: "The function of the military is ill-defined. Momentum is given to military programs beyond any utility." He cited the National Guard as an example. Kandel also saw the Army's reluctance to withdraw from Korea as part of an effort to preserve programs that had no defense utility. Kandel asserted that while the military may have some defense role, it also plays an important role as a supporter of political patronage. Kandel objected as well to the military research effort, which he saw as "distorting the national research process."

Several writers and producers objected to what they called "elitism" in the armed forces. One, Mort Lachman, called for an end to division of military personnel into commissioned and noncommissioned groups. General Dwight Eisenhower's warning against the "military-industrial complex" was cited by many writers and TV producers as the definitive word on the dangers of the military. Some opposed the volunteer army because, as they saw it, it tended to attract only unemployables. Others opposed the volunteer army because it allegedly created a military caste.

Of all the people I interviewed and all the people I dealt with in my own work in television, only one, the late Bruce Geller, even mentioned the existence of a possible Soviet threat in discussing the military. His opinion—that there was a real and definable threat—was almost unique, although, as noted above, there were frequent vague references to the "necessity" of having a military establishment. These, too, however, were outweighed by the comments of those who believed that the military existed mainly to provide work for military personnel.

Whence came this highly idiosyncratic notion of the reasons for the military and its role in America? To answer that question it is useful to note what was *not* said. For instance, not one person said that the military was plotting to take over the government. Similarly, not one person thought the military was trying to foment a nuclear war. There was concern about military men and businessmen as power centers in society, and there was concern about "scare tactics." But most of the worry was about the military's using resources to address what was widely perceived as a trumped-up problem. In addition, there was a complete absence of any belief that the military is a source or carrier of useful values or attitudes.

To believe that the military is serving no important defense function requires several corollary beliefs. One must also hold that the Soviet Union is not a military threat, either because of its own weakness or because of its disinclination to employ its strength. Or one must believe that the American military is so strong that its

requests for more arms are unjustified. That belief, however, requires a relative judgment about Soviet strength
or motives. Or one might believe that the present American system is so revolting that it should not be defended
and that military claims on labor to defend society are unjustified. However, no one interviewed expressed such a
feeling.

The main origin of the antimilitary feeling, then, might
be a failure to believe that the Soviet Union is a real
threat. Since the history of the world since World War II
seems to many to indicate that such a threat is real, the
universal (or near-universal) disbelief in such a threat
among the group I studied might have some origin other
than experience. It might be ideological, but the attitude
was held by TV writers and producers who believed ener-
getically in the capitalist society. It might be a vestige of
the odd 1960s concept that the military starts wars because it "likes" them, but not all of the people interviewed shared that bizarre New Left concept. Nor does
the feeling spring from anger or disillusionment with the
American government, since, as we will see, reactions
toward the government in general are far less negative.

Some explanation of the attitude towards the military
was offered by a high official of Tandem/TAT. "You have
to remember," he said, "that the people here are antiestablishment, and they see businessmen as part of the establishment, and they see the military as part of the establishment."

Indeed, extensions of this explanation yield an interesting thought. TV writers and producers who were
hostile toward business and businessmen were far more
hostile toward them than anyone was toward the mili-

tary. On the other hand, there were a few in the sample who felt highly favorably toward businessmen.

TV writers and producers deal with businessmen all the time. To some extent they are businessmen themselves. This familiarity may well lead to the intensity of feeling toward business in TV writing circles. Although the military is perceived like the businessmen as part of the establishment (one TV producer spun out for me a long web linking General Alexander Haig with Heinrich Himmler and Nelson Rockefeller!), TV writers hate the military far less intensively. If the TV writers were ever in the Army, it was usually a long time ago, in a cause they believed in. Thus, the TV writer sees the military as an object of hostility and anger, but only in a rather abstract form, since there has been no personal contact for a long time, if ever. Hence, the degree of hostility is far lower than it would otherwise be. Similarly, the TV writer does not see how he has ever been helped by the military, even though many Americans do, and thus he has none of the positive feeling toward the military that animates some wealthy TV writers and producers to feel kindly toward the business system (although such feelings are minority feelings).

There is also at least a hint of ethnic animosity in the feelings of TV writers toward the military. Whenever the subject came up in private conversations that were not part of formal interviews, the writers clearly thought of military men as clean-shaven, blond, and of completely WASP background. In the minds of a few of the people I interviewed, these blond officers were always a hair's breadth away from becoming National Socialists. They were thought of as part of an Aryan ruling class that actually or potentially repressed those of different ethnic backgrounds. But this was an opinion not widely held.

On television, then, there is a negative but usually not bitter attitude about the military. Military men are generally cast as stiff and bureaucratic, without much in the way of human feelings or human decency beyond a cartoon level. There is, of course, the exception of the superhero, but the basic military figure on television is not sympathetic.

The attitude about the military among TV writers and producers is basically that it exists mainly to feather its own nest. It does so by whipping up fears of an imaginary Soviet threat. At best, it is a grim necessity, whose members live in a world of their own with an archaic and unpleasant officer class dominating the ranks of an unemployable enlisted class. At worst, it is the reincarnated Wehrmacht.

Perhaps most interesting of all, neither on television nor in the minds of TV writers is there any belief that the military is the bearer of any useful value beyond its own self-preservation.

CHAPTER EIGHT

The Government on Television

ᴓᴓᴓ **O**FFICIALS of the federal government appear in prime-time TV shows in a variety of ways. On adventure shows, they can be either good or bad, competent or incompetent. On "The Six Million Dollar Man," the nonmilitary federal officials programming Steve Austin are usually intelligent, well-meaning people, often somewhat cowed by the military men. On "Police Story," federal narcotics officials are invariably overbearing and arrogant, looking down their well-financed noses at the lowly cop on the beat whom "Police Story" glorifies. They intrude into local police business and muddy up the case the Los Angeles Police Department was so laboriously making. In "Kojak," they may actually ruin one of Kojak's plans in order not to lose credit for a narcotics bust they had planned themselves.

(For some reason, the Drug Enforcement Administration in particular takes a beating on adventure shows. While other federal police agencies may use their enormous facilities to help locate fugitives or suspects, the DEA unfailingly messes things up with sloppy and self-serving work.)

On sitcoms, the attitudes toward the federal bureaucrat are more kindly. If a federal civil servant appears at all, he appears as a bumbler or a loud mouth, and hardly ever as evil. In "All's Fair," a continuing character was a United States senator from a midwestern state. He was ever full of farm homilies and good cheer. If he did anything even slightly wrong, he did it with a good-natured grin. Another running character was a White House speechmaker, patterned after a man known to the producers. He was primarily a gag writer, and although he was a political lightweight, he was never unkind.

On situation comedies, however, unlike adventure shows, federal officials put in few appearances, so that a broad sample does not exist. The rare federal inspector or bureaucrat is, however, generally a rather decent person, if a bumbler.

The attitude of the Hollywood TV writer and producer toward federal bureaucrats is similar to the depictions of bureaucrats on the screen in that they are generally thought of as ineffectual but decent human beings, and certainly no threat. That is also the attitude of those interviewed toward the bureaucracy in general, if the military, the CIA, the FBI, and the White House are excluded. Slight amusement, slight annoyance and slightly sympathetic tolerance—all of these sum up the feelings of TV writers and producers toward the bureaucracy.

Meta Rosenberg's comments were a good example of the general pattern. She saw the government as run by "faceless people, like the people at an insurance company." She asked rhetorically if they knew what they were doing and then answered her own question: "Absolutely not."

Rosenberg's feelings were different toward government at different levels. "Because people are in important jobs, that does not mean they are competent. There are decent people in government, but the problem is with the leadership." She saw the career civil servant as a fine man, competent and professional, while politicians, the FBI, and the CIA were corrupt and needed to be watched.

Stanley Kramer, too, believed that if one went beyond political excess, the government was a "gloriously imperfect piece of machinery." In spite of its inefficiency, the government did well, Kramer said. Bureaucrats, he noted, were "filled with an inadequate and frustrated desire to make it work better." Jim Brooks and Allen Burns had a similar view. They saw the government as generally incompetent but filled with well-meaning people. Jerry Thorpe also saw the government as incompetent and cumbersome, in need of streamlining, but well-intentioned. (Many of the people I interviewed had either friends or relatives in the bureaucracy in Washington and referred to them fondly. This phenomenon was completely absent in discussions of businessmen or the military or police or criminals.)

A statement remarkable for its mildness and lack of animosity about the government came from William Blinn. "It's like the Army," he said, "you only hear about it when it screws up. It's not to be loved or admired, but expected to do its job. We never hear about the good things government has done because no one bothers to report or read good news any more. The government is in the middle ball park. It's doing all right. I personally don't feel affected by it. I don't relate to the process. I live in the suburbs and feel no sense of government. The closest I get to having a sense of the government is watching the roads get built."

Some of the writers were almost positive about the government. Bob Weiskopf, for instance, said that he believes the government "is as competent as any large organization."

There was a substantial vein of negative comment about the government bureaucracy too, however. Little of it was bitter. Rather, it most often came across as a lament. Some of it was obviously relevant only to a limited social stratum. Mort Lachman was especially annoyed because the government "makes everyone in the country have to hire a tax attorney and an accountant." Lachman, along with Bob Schiller and others, cited the post office as an example of how poorly the government runs things, although he added that he thought many civil servants were highly idealistic. Bruce Geller said without qualification that the bureaucracy was "costly, overblown, and bloated."

Charlie Hauck had an interesting comparison to make about the federal government. "Any eleemosynary institution," he said, "has a problem keeping score, while profit-making institutions can keep score very easily. So federal agency heads add to their staffs. That's supposed to be an indication of progress. The better corporations have lean staffs. In corporations, all the attention is paid to the producers. In the government, there are few producers—very few."

The sum of it is that the people interviewed generally believed that the government was working in an inefficient way, although in principle it had its good points. The producers and writers also said that there were many good people in the government, if one left the top rungs of the ladder and the military and intelligence services out of the calculation. Even when expressing disappointment in the performance of the government, the writers and producers did so without anger or outrage.

And that, perhaps, is the most noteworthy finding about the government. The interviews were done at a time when antigovernment feeling was supposed to be running high in the nation. A president had just been elected whose main strength was supposed to be his having come from outside the governing establishment. In many cities, including Los Angeles, citizens were infuriated about government-mandated busing. (Not one person I spoke to mentioned busing in the context of the government or in any other way.)

People were supposedly angry about taxes, yet only one respondent even mentioned taxes, and that was in the context of having to hire a tax lawyer and accountant. There were no complaints about sloppy delivery of services (except for the post office) or the insolence of office. Although there have been outcries about the allegedly high level of federal and state pay, not one person mentioned governmental pay.

In short, the sample of creative people to whom I spoke was an eddy against the general national tide of anger at the government. Although no one had unmixed praise for the government, the mildness of the complaints was something like praising with faint damns. It represents a fundamentally kind attitude toward the government, which has been tarnished by the general perception of government's inefficiency. (Again, it is important to note that we are talking about the lower levels of bureaucracy, and not about presidents or directors of Central Intelligence.)

This is indeed the attitude about bureaucrats that comes across on television (if the DEA is excluded). They are amiable but bumbling, friendly but feckless, uncles and aunts who want to help but do not know how, like

the cheerful and friendly mail carrier who is always two
hours late, or the avuncular but stupid senator on "All's
Fair."

Why the uncommonly charitable attitude toward the
bureaucracy? It may have something to do with having
relatives in the bureaucracy. If writers can see that people
just like them are civil servants, then civil servants seem
less remote and frightening. No theory of conspiracy that
I heard ever involved civil servants, while many involved
businessmen and military men, which is an additional
reason why bureaucrats were not feared.

One might suspect a general prostatism bias on the
part of the writers and producers, but that would be hard
to substantiate. While many spoke of redistribution of
wealth in other contexts, no one said that the bureaucracy was well positioned to bring that about. No one said
that the government should make any of the major decisions about allocation and consumption or any of the
functions normally associated with a high degree of sta-
tism. The feelings of combined annoyance and tolerance
toward the government did not appear to reflect socialism, but rather an absence of bad feelings or of fear.

In sum, then, as a rule prime-time television presents
amiable but bumbling bureaucrats. TV writers and producers see them in a corresponding way—inefficient, incompetent, but not bad people. There was even a
frequent note of sympathy for the bureaucrat.

The noteworthy conclusion is that there were such *relatively* good feelings toward the government. The TV picture is usually the precise analogue of TV producers' and
writers' feelings about the world of bureaucrats.

CHAPTER NINE

Small Towns on Television

HERE IS a special genre of TV shows, cutting across situation comedy and adventure, which deals with small towns. That kind of show might be called "the city innocent in jeopardy" tale. Every adventure show that deals even once with small towns uses it, and every situation comedy set in the city eventually takes a stab at this type.

A family or individual from the city ventures out by car into the wilds of the countryside. He comes to a peaceful and lovely small town, such as might appear in a postcard of a typical small town. But something evil is afoot in the small town. Everyone, or almost everyone, in the small town is covering up something atrocious. To cover up, the town must enlist the police, who are always in the front line of evildoers in these situations. Often, the town must falsely imprison, and sometimes kill, for the secret of the town is critical and must be preserved from the city people at any cost. Eventually, some lone individual in the town comes to the rescue of the ensnared city dweller, and with the help of law forces from outside the small town, the evil is purged and the city people are free to go on their way—sadder but wiser about what really lurks out there in America's heartland.

On a recent "Kojak" (entitled "A Long Way From

Times Square"), Theo and his lieutenant went to a small
California town to bring back a fugitive from justice. In
that tiny town, it developed, the entire city police force
was on the take from gangsters and were sheltering the
witness to a Mafia rubout. One brave woman lawyer in
the town helped Kojak escape with his prisoner, but it
was a near thing.

On a recent "Cannon" (a series about an obese detective), the hero is ensnared in a town-wide plot to defraud
the outside world about murder, money, and raw sex.
Only when Cannon persuades the woman mayor of the
town of how base her way of life is does Cannon get the
help he needs to get the situation turned around. Mean-
while, he was constantly getting sniped at by a lunatic
scion of the local gentry.

On a two-part episode of "All's Fair", the ill-fated situation comedy on which I worked, the Washington, D.C.
heroes found themselves in a small town jail. The local
sheriff had locked them up as hostages to get a military base nearby reopened. The small town depended
on the military base to support a small empire of vice
which the police chief and the base C.O. were running
together.

Another part of the TV image of small towns is that
sexual mores there are more wicked, more primal than in
the city. A staple of the small-town episode of TV shows is
the small town sexpot trying, in vain, to seduce the good
guy from the city. Usually the girl in question is a combination of Daisy Mae Yokum and Carroll Baker's "Baby
Doll."

The most perfectly quintessential depiction of the small
town came in "The Rockford Files" episode in which Jim
Rockford, Malibu-based detective, found his car disabled

outside a small town. He was in for a series of shocks.
The sole local garage wanted to charge him several thousand dollars for repairing a minor ill. The police tried to
plant narcotics in his hotel room and then extort money
from him for his freedom. A teenager offered her body
and then someone rushed in and took pictures. It was
pretty damn tough until Jim Rockford enlisted the aid of
an old man who had inadvertently been left out of the
town scheme to fleece and blackmail passing motorists.
Eventually the conspirators were rounded up, depopulat-
ing the town, and even the ringleader, another woman
mayor, was sent to the pokey.

On "Good Times," when James, the hardworking but
luckless father of a poor black family, went off to Missis-
sippi to visit relatives, the first and last thing that happened to him was that he was killed in a mysterious automobile crash.

So it goes, over and over again. Small towns are
wicked, dangerous places. They are all slight variants of
Black Rock, Arizona, the small town in *Bad Day At
Black Rock* that was covering up a race murder. Even in
a superficially serene town, currents of murder and death
run deep and strong.

It is worth noting that there is one show set in a small
town in the 1930s—"The Waltons"—in which a highly
positive image of the small town comes across. There is
only one "Waltons" and it is set in a far-removed time
period. It is also much more frankly a sentimental journey
without any pretentions to reality than any other prime-
time show. Perhaps most important, it is *always* set in the
small town, and therefore the small town could not be an
evil conspiracy week after week unless "The Waltons"
were to become "The CBS Evening News."

On television, then, small towns take it on the chin over and over again, almost every week. As standard as the murdered go-go dancer who was a witness to an underworld murder and more frequent than the policeman's girlfriend killed by a psychopathic rapist, the small-town morality tale is a major genre of TV story.

This negative image of small towns is very much at odds with the way small towns have traditionally been viewed by American creative types. Since the era of Jefferson and before, small towns were the backbone of America, repositories of all that was good about America and treasuries of the solid values that have kept America strong and free. The cities were cesspools of corruption where innocent country boys and girls met ruinous fates. That image of small towns has, in fact, never died in literature. It is extremely weak among TV shows. Except in "The Waltons," good small towns usually do not exist, period. As television typecasts almost everything else, it has typecast small towns as bad places indeed.

Among the TV writers and producers I interviewed, I found a generally corresponding feeling about small towns. Although there were exceptions, there was, as a rule, a negative feeling also about the attitudes of people in small towns. Writers and producers spoke of the "narrowness" and "insularity" of small towns. Some spoke of their political conservatism, and never with approval. On the other hand, there was a feeling that small towns had certain virtues that big cities lacked, especially a feeling of community, of neighborliness. To some extent, this set of feelings is the conceptual analog of the TV picture—towns have superficial appeal with underlying unpleasantness, if not horror.

Stephen Kandel summed up the general feeling when

he said that he thought of "limitations, security, roots, boredom, routine, and provincialism" when asked about small towns.

Among the negative comments about small towns, Stanley Kramer's stood high. "My instinct," he said, "is to say that small towns are extremely reactionary. In strict pursuit of the clichès of America, they endanger America." Kramer saw small-town dwellers as "living in a certain way. Then they are jolted to believe there is a world plot gnawing at their own security." Kramer added that "some small towns represent all that is strong. But also, some small towns have attacked me." He explained that he had experienced a lot of small-town hostility while filming "Inherit The Wind," his movie about the Scopes trial.

Meta Rosenberg, who produces "The Rockford Files," sees small towns as having "probably a greater sense of community. People are together in one environment. People cling to each other." On the other hand, Rosenberg said, "Corruption can permeate a community which is small. In large cities, corruption and people are dissipated." Rosenberg also saw a political problem in small towns, in that people in small towns "are less politically aware and more conservative." When asked if she considered small towns frightening, Rosenberg at first said "No," and then added, "Jesus, they did vote for Nixon."

Allen Burns and Jim Brooks, the superheroes of TV comedy writing, had mixed feelings about small towns. Both thought that small towns held a romantic illusion for them, although Brooks said that the worst thing about small towns ". . . is that you can't get laid there." (He is a famous joke writer.) In a more serious comment, Brooks found no intellectual stimulation in small towns.

"They might be nice places to retreat to, but ultimately tedious to live in." While Burns thought that small towns were not particularly wholesome (he preferred London), Brooks found them definitely wholesome.

Burns was particularly concerned that small towns might have people who were against gun control. He is in favor of stricter gun control. (He had, in fact, recently put a gun control sticker on his car and wondered if that might make him a target of people with guns.)

Charlie Hauck gave small towns a mixed and thoughtful review. "I do not associate them with cleanliness. Actual small towns are not that clean, although fantasy ones are." He spoke of coal towns and steel towns and simply shook his head. "Small towns can be closed societies. They're wholesome places to live if you're in synchronization with the prevailing mores. There is a certain degree of intolerance." Hauck saw small towns as definitely "not dangerous." In Hauck's opinion, they have supplied the creative talent of America.

One of Hauck's colleagues, who did not want his name to appear, saw small towns as cultural backwaters, "the kinds of places where the Ku Klux Klan could grow today . . . right now." In an interesting aside, that writer attributed whatever progress he might admit that small towns had made away from their "witch-burning past" to television and the movies.

The theme of limits in small towns was stressed again by Jerry Thorpe. "When I think of the people in small towns," he said, "I think of people who are somewhat limited in their exposure, people who never see an ocean, never see a ballet."

The notion that people in small towns are different from people in big cities was frequently heard during my interviews. When such comparisons were made, they were almost invariably to the advantage of people in the cities. David Begelman, for instance, saw small towns as "difficult places to get used to unless you were born there or lived in that environment. . . . People in cities are more mobile. They have a greater interest in things outside their own purview. In small towns, people are limited to their immediate purview." Begelman noted that within this area, Southerners were relatively more restricted than others.

Within the general text of negative comments about small towns' reactionary politics and cultural insularity, there was a strong subtext of appreciation for the "togetherness" and safety of the small town. Thad Mumford paid a fairly typical left-handed compliment when he saw small towns as "sterile, with no chance to grow, but safe in terms of violence."

Matthew Rapf, a producing power at Universal and producer of "Kojak," thinks of the pretty small towns near Hanover, New Hampshire where he went to college as "good places, wholesome and safe."

Bob Schiller, who grew up partly in a small town, loved the neighborliness and gossip of small towns. "I like to see people's roots, and you can see the roots in a small town." In a rather standard note, though, Schiller pointed out that "some towns east of Los Angeles are hotbeds of right-wing thought."

Mort Lachman saw small towns as safe and "affectionate." However, like everyone else, he saw a certain narrowness and insularity and noted that "small towns are not any more wholesome than anyplace else."

A strong feeling runs through the people I talked to that small towns are pretty to look at, secure in terms of physical assault, but different and somewhat frightening politically. Although a few of the people to whom I spoke said they would like to live in a small town, even they had qualifications that would clearly make it impossible. (For the hardy commuter, there are small towns within commuting distance of Hollywood.) There was, in short, some feeling of warmth toward the small town, but it did not run deep. Further, it was clear to me that no one I talked to had a powerful affinity for life in small towns or considered them comfortable for him or her personally.

Partly, this is a tautology. People who have lived for some time in large cities have shown a preference for life in the city. It would be surprising to interview people who lived in the city and find that they would prefer to live in the country. Such is the situation with Hollywood TV writers and producers.

But there are other reasons for the discomfort and resentment directed at small towns. For one thing, most of the writers and producers originally come from large eastern cities or from Los Angeles, and they are uncomfortable with the whole concept of small towns. Like Stanley Kramer, they are uneasy generally in thinking about what might lurk out there between the Atlantic and the Pacific. It is largely *terra incognita,* and like everyone else in the world, TV writers and producers are frightened by what they do not know.

There is also an ethnic difference that frightens some. The Hollywood TV writer tends generally, although not always, to be Jewish or Italian or Irish, and he sees people in the small towns as not being ethnic at all. He sees them, moreover, as not being friendly toward ethnics, especially Jews. Gary Marshal summed up the problem succinctly: "I've heard a lot of stories about Jews being beat up in small towns." Marshal added that while he was Italian himself, "I've heard a lot of stories about small towns beating up Jews and blacks. This is not paranoia. It really happened. There are a lot of dumb, violent people in small towns." Marshal explicitly stated the fears many writers and producers had about small towns when they spoke of the "narrowness" or insularity of those areas. And, of course, it could hardly be more natural for people who fear that they might be "beat up" in small towns because of their race to feel some anger toward them.

Further, there is the political problem. By and large, the people in Hollywood TV production are not conservative or right wing, whatever else they may be. The thought of a hinterland full of small towns who voted for Nixon, as Meta Rosenberg said, makes them uneasy. They see a strong challenge to the brand of politics they favor, and, quite naturally, that affronts them. Politics in a small town are not only different, but to a large extent they are also incomprehensible. Many interviewees echoed, in different ways, David Begelman's comments about how different small-town people are. Perhaps the most confusing difference is about politics, since most of the people I talked to consider an act such as voting for Nixon utterly outlandish.

There are specific political differences too, as well as the general perceived liberal-conservative dichotomy. Allen Burns' worries about gun control opponents in small towns was only one of several remarks—all fearful and uncomplimentary—about people who display rifles and shotguns in the back windows of pickup trucks.

A variety of differences and fears separate the Hollywood TV writer and producer from the small town as he sees it. Fear of violence and animosity being directed at him because of race or religion, fear and lack of comprehension about the politics of small-town people, and a generalized fear of the unknown produce a powerful wave of dislike of small towns in the minds of TV writers and producers, which makes itself felt in TV programming.

And there are other reasons as well. Jerry Thorpe pointed out that the small-town-as-lair-of-evil-conspirators plot has been popular since *The Ox-Bow Incident.* By now, he said, it is a staple dramatic form and simply runs on its own momentum. That, too, cannot be discounted. In TV writing, as in other forms of life, clichès take on a life of their own and continue to run because producers and writers know that by now a comfortable niche has been worn in the viewer's mind.

To some extent, the revolt of the 1960s and 1970s against industrialism and urban values has made itself felt in television. While the bad small town is still common fare, there are extremely recent stirrings of change. In TAT, Norman Lear's production company, two shows set in small towns have appeared within the last two years— "Mary Hartman, Mary Hartman" and "Fernwood 2 Night." In both shows, what Marx called "the idiocy of rural life" comes across powerfully. The small Ohio town of Fernwood, not quite rural and not quite industrial, is full of bigots, Klansmen, quacks, hillbillies, and religious frauds. However, there is clearly a great deal of affection for Fernwood, and sometimes it has occurred to me that Fernwood represents a kind of psychic resting place for the writers in Norman Lear's stable, as well as an outlet for a yearning for small town life. Further, the emphasis in many commercials—which often are culturally ahead of programming—on small-town values and "naturalness" may be a sign that the monolith of antismall-town feeling is breaking up. Still, these are no more than straws in the wind.

At present, the picture is one of superficial affection for small towns, coupled with a powerful anger against the threat and the differentness that TV writers and producers see coming from small towns. The cathode ray product is the small town where bad things happen to the city slicker-innocent.

CHAPTER TEN

Big Cities on Television

HE BIG CITY that makes its appearance on prime time is either New York or Los Angeles, with a few exceptions. Every adventure show except "Streets of San Francisco" and "Starsky and Hutch" is set in Los Angeles or New York at the time of this writing. Situation comedies are supposedly spread around the country in many medium-size cities such as "Mary Tyler Moore's" Minneapolis, "One Day At A Time's" Indianapolis, "All's Fair's" Washington, D.C., "Phyllis's" San Francisco, and so forth. But when the overwhelming unseen ambiance of the big city is called for, it will be New York, as in "The Jeffersons," "All In The Family," "Maude" (a suburb of New York), "Rhoda," and others.

In the geography of television, Los Angeles and New York are far more significant than the rest of the country. In sharp contrast to the TV image of small towns, Los Angeles and New York come across as places of superficial violence and jeopardy but underlying decency and compassion. This comes out in the most obvious of all possible ways—the infinite variety of the city. While many people who are violent and evil are shown, many people who are stout and fair characters also put in appearances. On any episode of "Kojak" or "Columbo" or "Starsky and Hutch" there are violent, desperate men and women, but there are also plenty of shopkeepers who saw the crime and will talk, impoverished roommates who will risk everything to catch the murderer of their topless-dancer roommates, widows in tenements who will inform on the syndicate to save their grandsons from becoming junkies, and so on. Never is there the universal conspiracy that we see in small towns, in which every single person is caught up in something evil.

On "All In The Family" there is the usual plethora of big-city ailments and complaints, but there are also kindly people waiting to lend a hand. There is never a problem with boredom. Something is always happening to refresh the spirit of the weary city dweller. A tired Archie may end up his moonlighting at home by finding that he has just given mouth-to-mouth resuscitation to a transvestite. The Jeffersons may be constantly put down in their strivings to become true upper-class black bourgeoisie, but there are always more chances for them to make fools of themselves. Opportunities grow lushly in the concrete jungle.

In the city, moreover, even the evil people, the gangsters and the criminals are recognizable. They may have some mannerism, some tic that betrays them as being one of us, unlike the outlandish strangers we see in the small towns. Nowhere in the city are the unapproachable small-town cops, utterly rigid and unbending in their commitment to wickedness, beyond the realm even of communication with people from the big city. When the big-city criminal is captured he makes a wisecrack or an animal groan that tells us he is one of us, a suffering human, and not the robot SS man of the small town.

And while innocent people suffer and die in the big city, as well as in the small town, often the victims are not quite as innocent in the big city. There are more cases of the bad killing their own. There is menace in both places, but there is less menace, and a less conspiratorial menace, in the big city.

The feelings of TV writers and producers toward the big city, which is always either New York or Los Angeles, are mixed. There is almost always a powerful note of affection for the bigger city, for its energy, its electricity, and its opportunities, combined with laments about how it has gone to the dogs. About Los Angeles, comments are far more narrow. If there is criticism of Los Angeles, it takes the form of rather gentle wrist slapping about its quietness or supposed lack of inspiration. When Los Angeles comes up, in fact, it is frequently described as a collection of small towns that make up a large city, and so it escapes both the positive and negative comments about both big cities and small towns. Instead, people who have moved to Los Angeles from the East have a new genre of complaints that center around the general term "laid-back."

And yet, no deep distinction occurs in TV shows set in New York or Los Angeles about the quality of urban life. Basically, any show set in Los Angeles might just as well be set in New York and vice versa. To the TV viewer, except for the palm trees and other surface styles, it is all the same city.

That may be because almost everyone interviewed had spent substantial time in both New York and Los Angeles, and perhaps the experience of the cities had blended together to form one unified city *for writing purposes,* even though for purposes of recollection, New York can be remembered as different from Los Angeles.

Still, there were substantial gradations of feeling about New York and Los Angeles. Stanley Kramer's feeling was among the more negative. Speaking of New York and of big cities in general as models of New York, Kramer said, "The problem is ghettoes. Cities are places which no longer work as communities. They are unpleasant. The air is bad. The transportation is bad. The safety factor is dangerous. The outer shell of sophistication does not show the city as it really is. It's a façade." However, Kramer noted, if a person grows up in the city and survives it, he may become stronger. "But you might not want your children to grow up in it."

Stephen Kandel thinks of New York as "a dinosaur, a structural failure . . . sheer unlivability, with a tremendous lag between the government structure and reality." Kandel thought that New York, in which he once worked as a welfare bureaucrat, was not wholesome, not safe, and not a good place for a family.

David Begelman saw big cities having "pockets of affluence in oceans of poverty." Bob Schiller sounded the note of lamentation for past glories that echoed through many answers about New York. "New York City is the most vibrant city, if not in the world, at least in the United States. But you have to take a lot of crap. It's not even nice to visit it. It's a constant struggle. All of the horrible things that are happening to our society are happening there. It's a faded jewel. It's Gomorrah to Las Vegas' Sodom. There's no humanity in New York." Schiller said that the minute he gets to the airport he starts pushing and shoving, literally and figuratively. However, Schiller said, every young person should spend a year or two in New York. It's the most exciting of American cities, he felt.

For Mort Lachman, an anecdote summed up New York. "I think of a lady at Sardi's who punched me with

her elbow to get to the maître d'." Gary Marshal, a native
of New York, also had epigrammatic thoughts about the
Big Apple: "It's a dangerous place. People hit me there
when I was growing up."

As mentioned above, there were also some extremely
kind words for New York, especially from people who
had recently lived there. Jim Brooks said that he felt very
much more comfortable in New York than in Hollywood.
Allen Burns called New York "invigorating, exciting. . . .
Everybody's reading." Brooks thinks he is actually smar-
ter in New York. Both Burns and Brooks note that the life
of "Rhoda," set in New York City, is considerably more
frantic than the life of "Mary Tyler Moore," set in Minneapolis.

A series of highly flattering remarks about New York
came from Charlie Hauck. "I like it more and more," he
said. "I've never lived there, but each time I go there I
have more money than I had before." Hauck did not
think of New York as a dangerous place. He never felt
afraid there. "It's not a wholesome place," Hauck said,
"because it's not relaxed enough to be wholesome. What
it lacks in wholesomeness, though, it makes up for in
creative energy." Hauck added, "You can almost feel
New York when you're there."

Matthew Rapf saw New York as "an exciting place,
one of the most exciting places in the world." Rapf spent
a lot of time there in 1938 through 1942, but he said that
the city has changed and deteriorated a great deal since
then. "Culturally, it is far more stimulating than most
American cities."

Thad Mumford had the highest praise for New York. "I
love it," he said. "I'm crazy about it. I miss it greatly. You
can see all kinds of people. There is intelligence, bright-

ness, life—real life as opposed to a fairy-tale fantasy land
like Los Angeles. You have to deal with the city and that
keeps you going."

Mumford's comments about Los Angeles led naturally
into the feeling about that city. "There is no energy in Los
Angeles. No life force." Others saw Los Angeles as "a
collection of small towns" (Bob Schiller), "a place that
doesn't demand much of you" (Jim Brooks), "a quiet
place, but much better for raising a family than New
York" (almost everyone), and "so spread out that there's
no sense of community" (William Blinn).

There is hardly any thought that Los Angeles is a dangerous or unwholesome place like New York, or a place
of high excitement or stimulation, also like New York.
Comments about Los Angeles, like the city itself, tend to
be far more relaxed and "laid-back."

The perception of New York as the ultimate American
big city, an exciting and lively place laced with deterio-
ration, danger, and despair, is apparently the result of
simple observation of New York and an affection for the
city that will not die despite the filth, the street killings, the
junkies, the high prices, the cheating, the dirty air, and the
other realities of New York life.

New York, as the hometown of the writers or their
parents or their grandparents, in most cases is remembered fondly. It is a place where, even if the writer might
be a stranger today, he once was not a stranger. The
writers and producers are city people, and even if the city
has changed, they retain an affection for it. It was never
completely *terra incognita,* like small southern or southwestern towns.

Now the writers and producers live in Los Angeles,
which lacks the excitement of New York but which is a

good place to raise children, according to the writers and producers, although there is conflicting evidence.

And so there is the image of New York on the screen as a dangerous place but one full of resources, an image corresponding to the writers' and producers' thoughts. And blending in with that image is Los Angeles, laid back a little but, on the screen, still the psychic re-creation of a city much like New York with palm trees. The thought of New York has such strength in the writers' minds that it becomes the dominant cityscape of the air, even if —visually—the scene is clearly set in Los Angeles.

The affection that TV writers and producers feel for New York comes across clearly in shows set in Los Angeles. A person who has lived in both places can easily see that even if a Chicano is shown lounging next to a palm tree, New York is in the writer's mind. And since the TV writer feels a deep affection for New York, his portrait of the city, whether ostensibly Los Angeles or New York, is suffused with a warmth utterly lacking in portraits of small towns on television, even as we see the filth of Times Square.

CHAPTER ELEVEN

The Rich on Television

⮌⮌⮌ **O**N TELEVISION, both the rich and the poor make appearances, as they often do in real life. Rich people seldom have shows exclusively devoted to them, but they appear on other shows about the less affluent. On the whole, the rich people on prime time are not beautiful people. While they may be lovely superficially, they will be scheming, unhappy people who would just as soon commit murder as buy an original Renoir. They will have contempt for anyone who is not rich. And they have gotten their money by doing something we might just as well not know about—unless it was inherited. If they do not fit those categories, they will be effeminate, prissy, stuffy types, Lord and Lady Fauntleroys of the first water.

Often, there are hilarious bits of Hollywood nuance thrown in. On a recent "Kojak," a stinking rich Harvard grad was the object of a murder plan. He spoke with a stilted accent, moved his hands in swishy motions, and announced that his only concern was protecting the environment. (That was right on target.) However, he appeared dressed in tight-fitting hip-huggers and a body shirt unbuttoned to the waist like a Hollywood gigolo.

On every single episode of "Columbo" a murder has been committed by a plutocrat. Invariably, the murderer lives in a big, gloomy house and talks to Columbo as if his mouth were full of mush. While looking down his nose at Columbo's style (or lack of it), the rich person tries to cover his own guilt with sheer condescension.

If Rockford, of "The Rockford Files," is invited to find the missing daughter of an industrialist, you can be sure that the industrialist has been up to no good and that the daughter, in revulsion at the way she got her Camaro, has run off.

When a rich person appears on a sitcom, trouble follows. On "All's Fair," the rich people who visited Richard Barrington, the columnist, were invariably right-wing kooks and sex fiends. On "Maude," they are generally businessmen out to humiliate Walter, Maude's husband, while trying to be sanctimonious.

Sometimes, strange words are put into a rich man's mouth on television. For instance, on a recent "Kingston: Confidential" Kingston confronted a rich man who said, "He who builds a factory builds something more important than a church, for he builds a temple to the greatest god of all—capitalism." This is supposed to be a quote from J. P. Morgan, which it almost is, but people on television rarely quote famous men. Since they are so strange, however, rich people can do it.

Rich women on television are a familiar type. They dart in and out of the house in tennis outfits, contemptuously but lustfully eyeing the shabby private detective who might be there. They order their servants around, talk about parties and balls, and generally bring Scarlett O'Hara to Beverly Hills.

This is far from a totally negative attitude toward the rich. It is, for example, not as venomous as the attitude toward businessmen. Some rich people on television, even if they are ridiculous, are not evil, which is a step up from the businessman. Similarly, I have not seen any rich TV people who were Nazis, as some military men are. Nevertheless, the basic portrait of the rich man is highly uncomplimentary on television. It is worth examining in detail the attitude of TV writers and producers toward wealth and money in general, to see what kind of fit there might be between the portrait of money incarnate on television and the attitudes of the Hollywood TV writers and producers toward money and the acquisition of it.

First, it might be interesting to review the money situation of the people we are talking about. In a word, it is extremely good. A writer called in to write a 23-minute situation comedy might well get over $5,000 for a thirty-five-page document (with wide margins). A good writer under contract to a production company for a show will hardly ever get less than $2,000 a week and usually more. For a teleplay of an adventure show, which might be 50 minutes long, a writer could get between $12,000 and $25,000.

Producers get considerably more. A man who has created an idea and produced a prime-time half-hour situation comedy might get $7,000 to $10,000 a week. For an adventure show lasting one hour, the pay would be slightly more than double the sitcom amount. If the show is successful and goes into reruns or foreign sales, the producers and writers can get substantial additional amounts.

Should the show last enough seasons—usually four or five—to go into syndication, the producer gets a bonanza that could be in the millions. If a producer is inventive enough, hardworking enough, and lucky enough to produce more than one show, he can simply multiply all his fees by the number of shows he produces. Further, if a producer owns the rights to several shows that are ripe for syndication, he is suddenly sitting on top of Kuwait. A few producers in Hollywood can confidently expect fees for syndication rights in the hundreds of millions of dollars.

It should be understood, then, that we are talking about a well-paid group of individuals. Nevertheless, they are generally quite uncomfortable about money, and they do not see themselves as rich people. In fact, they perceive a huge gap between themselves and those they see as the rich, and they are not happy about it. Moreover, one gets the impression that they are not quite certain how their own modest degree of good fortune came upon them.

The interviewees were asked how people get rich in America, and a few of them rambled on about money and their lives. The consensus idea, interestingly enough, was that people get rich through the operation of the capitalist system. Lee Rich's speech is a good example.

"You're never going to get rich working for somebody," he said. "You may get a big salary, pension, or profit-sharing. The only way you're going to get rich today is when you're in business for yourself. You can be comfortably well off working for someone else, but you won't get rich. Working for yourself, you'll either get very rich or poor, depending on how hard you want to work, whether you're at the right place at the right time, how bright you are, and most important, how lucky you are.

"There's too much going to the government when you're on salary. If you're on salary at $200,000 a year, then your life style is living to that salary. If you're getting that much money, then your life is dependent on it. You're not going to continue living the way you were when you were making $50,000. You live in a different manner on a bigger salary. So of that $200,000 you're going to keep very little of it. Forget becoming rich unless you're working for yourself or have stock options."

Many people interviewed used what some might think of as extremely high salaries as examples of how little money people who are not working for themselves will make. Two hundred thousand dollars in salary might, some may say, make a person rich automatically. But the people in Hollywood have higher standards, since their salary framework starts at about $2,000 a week.

The capitalist concept, or, more properly, the concept of individual enterprise, was on Mort Lachman's mind as well in considering how to get rich: "There are about ten ways you can do it," he said. "Not by early to bed, early to rise. It must be in the form of selling or producing. You have to gamble. You have to receive a profit, not a salary. Or be a brilliant inventor. Or inherit money. There are many, many ways. But you must be an owner and not an employee."

David Begelman had similar ideas about accumulating riches in America. "The best way," he said, "is to accumulate substantial sums before taxation. Now, to become well-to-do, you have to have investments in growth stocks or else develop a small company and then sell it. Saving money out of income is just about impossible. Also, the corporate managerial class has opportunities because of stock options."

Charlie Hauck had the most succinct answer about how to get rich in America: "Manufacture something and sell it for cost plus 5 percent. It takes a second-rate idea and a first-rate man. It takes good skill at marketing."

There was a raft of comments about how to become

rich that suggested hard work plus something that is rarely taught in economics classes. "You can't get rich in America unless you cheat a little. The tax structure doesn't permit getting rich. If it did, we'd be much more capable of making money and keeping it," said the late Bruce Geller. "In my business, I don't know many people who have risen through struggling or competence. I know a few people who have gotten ahead through their social status and knowing the right people. Luck, timing, and fortuitous circumstances play a great part in making it. I consider myself quite good at what I do, but I also consider myself lucky. Having the right idea at the right time [helps]. I know how to write scripts that give people the big feeling," Geller added.

The concept of luck as crucial, second perhaps only to cheating, came up again and again. Gary Marshal said that luck was the most important factor in getting rich, "including upbringing, heritage, and so forth." He added that "there's also an intangible—drive, working hard." Marshal quoted with approval a local politician who said, "The harder I work, the luckier I get." Then Marshal noted that "some do it in Machiavellian ways. The really rich started with it. For rock stars, it's luck." Marshal had a sanguine thought about the enrichment process: "Society loves to make people rich. That's great. But people are made rich for the wrong reasons—for singing, not for curing cancer. There is a system of making people rich. It has to do with exposure and popularity. But again, the real rich are those who started with it, like the Hunts of Texas, for example."

A viewpoint that combined several elements and added a solution to the problem of taxation came from Bob Schiller. "One of the best ways [to get rich] is by tak-

ing risks and having smart tax attorneys. I think that speculation in America—land speculation, stock speculation—is probably the most common way of amassing a
fortune, and I suspect that it is proved by statistics. The
best way is the increase in value of one piece of property
relative to another. And there are tax laws that shelter
some of this by making it capital gains.

"There are other ways. Certainly, you can't discount
ingenuity. I can think of several examples of people who
are ingenious—Mr. Land of Polaroid, for example."
(Schiller then spoke at length about the unfairness of laws
that allegedly treat wealthy crooks more leniently than
poor ones.)

Few people indeed thought of wealth as coming from
hard work and decency alone. According to Bob Weiskopf, "You get rich, I guess, by luck. You can win a lot-
tery in New York and get rich. That's one way. Pure luck.
You can be shrewd and sharp and apparently there's still
some ways to make money by being sharper than the
guy next to you. But I think the Horatio Alger syndrome
is gone—almost entirely."

A similar view came from Douglas Benton: "People get
rich by an astounding streak of good luck. Five people
will go on the same path and one of them will make a
million dollars and four of them will go broke. That's
because what the one man owned was just what the
public wanted. The public wanted a hula hoop so the guy
got rich. I don't think hard work or initiative will make you
rich. It might provide you with a good living, but that's
all."

Those who did think that hard work could lead to material well-being never thought hard work was sufficient
to garner real, substantial wealth. At best, as Jerry Thorpe

said, "personal industry" could ensure being "well-to-do." (Thorpe saw inheritance as the surest route to wealth.) One man, Matthew Rapf, had about the most positive view of the utility of hard work as a means to riches. "Hard work, plus guts, plus taking chances will do it," he said.

Few had as negative an attitude about how big money is made in America as Thad Mumford. "How do people get rich in America?" he asked. "It beats me. It's impossible to get rich by saving money. You cannot start at zero. You must have a good-paying job. It helps to come from money. You get familiar with the ways of making money." And then Mumford noted, "The whole idea of making money changes a person's attitude. It makes people callous towards other people. You cannot make a lot of money without stepping on people."

None of those questioned, amazingly enough, said that the way to get rich was to have a good idea and make it into a network TV show. None of them said that doing anything in the entertainment line was a way to make money, although many of those interviewed were at least millionaires.

The writers and producers, in many ways business-men, differentiated themselves sharply from business-men. Similarly, although in many ways rich, they differentiated themselves sharply from the rich. They obviously thought of the Rockefellers or the Hunts when they thought of "rich," just as they thought of the board chairman of ITT when they thought of "businessman."

If they had made a lot of money, they tastefully did not mention it. If they did, they belittled the entire concept of money as valuable. Leonard Goldberg, a top TV mogul, had a fascinating view of the world and of money. He ap-

parently saw a world of people who own major TV production companies: "Money has no value anymore. You
could charge $5,000 for a shirt in a store and people
would buy it. Most people don't even look at their bills.
Their business manager pays them. They have no idea of
what things cost. I, personally, don't carry money, except
for a dollar. When you have cash in your pocket, instead
of credit cards, you get a sense of the transaction. But
when you sign for everything, money loses its value. It
means something when you have money in your pocket
and you spend it and see it disappearing.

"People don't buy cars; they lease them. Or the company leases the car for you. I just found out the other day
how much the car I'm driving costs. Fifteen thousand
dollars. It's leased for me. That's absurd. I'm also de-
tached from my salary. I no longer see my weekly pay-
check. It goes to my business manager. It felt good to
cash my check each week, to see and feel the stack of
dollars I had worked for. And I had to weigh what I
bought in terms of what I had. Now, I never see what I
make. Even my bills go to my business manager. He's the
only one who knows whether I'm winning or losing.
Money definitely affects the way you live. Buying a single
item used to be so meaningful. When I used to spend $5
for a tie, it had to be a terrific tie, and I'd take time decid-
ing which one to buy. It's been a long time since I've had
$15 in my pocket."

The extremely articulate Leonard Goldberg clearly explained what it was like both to have a lot of money and
to feel some considerable unease about it. And in a pleasant interview, he revealed the situation of the highly-paid
Hollywood writer or producer for television. While he
may be making money, while he may even have accumu-

lated a lot of money, he feels extremely uneasy and uncomfortable about it. His feelings and sympathies do not
lie naturally with the plutocracy, which he sees as an alien
group making money through ownership of patents or
through inheritance.

Rich people, according to the producers and writers,
make money in ways that they know nothing of. Moreover, most of the ways have an unsavory tinge. Clearly, it
is unlike writing or producing a TV show. There is little
kinship between a rich industrialist and a rich TV producer, even though the TV producer might make more
money.

Conversations off the record with writers and producers made it clear that rich people, like businessmen
and military officers, are a breed apart—lean, trim, blond,
and dangerous, and not at all like them.

If TV people have money, they see themselves as
lucky, working-class types, not plutocrats, and their sympathies will never lie with the heirs and heiresses, even
though their children may be heirs and heiresses. TV
writers and producers see rich people as different from
themselves in some way other than the possession of
money. It has something to do with ethnicity, political
leanings, education, background, and probably other
things as well. However, no amount of money in the
bank will link TV writers and producers, who have made
their money by the sweat of their brows plus a little luck,
with people who man the fortress of the rich, who got it
"by stepping on someone else."

Additionally, many, if not most, of the TV writers and
producers I interviewed thought of themselves as artists.
Traditionally, even artists who have struck it rich do not
think of themselves in the same league as their patrons

and patronesses. Further, artists often think of themselves as against the establishment and far removed from it.

Obviously, it would be difficult for artists and antiestablishment figures to think of themselves as akin to those who are the essence of the establishment. The fact that TV writers and producers are the inheritors and captains of a powerful establishment of their own simply does not count in their minds. Perhaps everyone thinks he is outside the establishment, no matter who he is. In any event, people who write for television and produce for television certainly do. They are workers, albeit well-paid workers. They are a million miles from the "400" in their minds.

This feeling carries over to the TV screen. Rich people on television are stuffy, cunning establishment figures, either evil or pompous—sometimes both. They do not have that sympathetic aspect television gives to policemen, for instance, or to poor people. Rich people on television are alien creatures, as they are in the minds of those who create TV shows.

CHAPTER TWELVE

The Poor on Television

ALONG TIME AGO,
many people thought that poor people were poor because they deserved to be. A flaw of laziness or shiftlessness kept some people poor, while the energetic, imaginative, and disciplined poor soon entered middle-class or upper-middle-class life.

That image of the poor is by and large long gone from American thought, and it is completely gone from television. If there is any sort of people who are unequivocally loved on television, it is the poor. They do no wrong, are always either heroes or victims, have great senses of humor, and are simply wonderful people.

In comedy, there are several shows about poor people. "Good Times" has a cast of poor black people in the Chicago ghetto. The family has several poor black friends who occasionally appear. They are always kindly and considerate human beings. If trouble intrudes, it is in the human form of someone who is not poor. A pimp wants to take advantage of the children. A businessman wants to take advantage of the children. Someone with money wants to take advantage of people who don't have any money.

"What's Happening" shows a kind of black "Our

Gang," slightly older and with a mother. They are mis-
chievous kids, but they are damn good kids. If they do
anything even slightly overmischievous, their mama
"whups" them. But basically the kids, despite their lack
of middle-class amenities, are young saints.

Poor people on adventure shows fare just as well, if not
better. Poor people are generally cast as bystanders to violent crimes. While suspicion might occasionally fall upon
one of them, it is lifted as soon as we are past the third
commercial break. A classic example, cited before, appeared on a recent "Streets of San Francisco" episode
and showed a murder on a campus. The most likely suspect was an impoverished Chicano who had already
committed an armed robbery. In fact, the murderer was
the dead girl's lesbian roommate-lover.

On "Starsky and Hutch," a black street criminal may
have been distantly connected with a murder, (—he
stuck in the knife—) but the strings have been pulled by
Mr. Big in a three-piece suit, and it will be the poor man
who blows the whistle on the gangster chieftain.

A poor person on television never lives on welfare. A
poor person on television never, never, never is voluntar-
ily poor. A poor person on television is always neat and
well-groomed. A poor person on television always tells
the truth. And so on, and so on, and so on. (I am re-
minded of the pitiful mother of the "downstairs" class on
"The Young and the Restless." While that show is a soap
opera and thus not described here, it is worth noting that
the patient, wise, and kind creature had an air of long-
suffering weariness and nobility that makes Mother
Teresa of Calcutta look like Diane von Furstenburg.)

There is some feeling among the American people that
occasionally a poor person might take welfare payments

he is not entitled to, or might loot, or might simply not want to work—because society has so demoralized him. That point of view never puts in an appearance on television. The poor person who is a cheat, like the poor person who is a criminal, just is not there. If, *in extremis,* a poor person has done something wrong, he has been forced to do it by the pig power structure. For no other group on television is there such evident sympathy as appears for the poor.

Among TV writers and directors, sympathy and compassion for the poor is also more pronounced than for any other group. In an America riddled with flaws, great and small, the poor stand out as blameless and pure as the driven snow. Only one writer expressed even the slightest unhappiness with poor people. For most interviewees, poor people were trapped by a world they never made—doomed to suffer so that others might be rich.

Bob Weiskopf's comments were unusually apt but quite representative. It might be useful to follow the dialogue as it was recorded.

Q. Why are people poor in America?
A. Because I don't think the system could function if everyone was well off.
Q. What do you mean?
A. I think you have to have poor people in a capitalist society.
Q. Why?
A. To exploit. The rich people can't exploit each other. Consequently they always exploit the poor.

Bob Schiller gave a similar answer: "To be very easy and very socialistic [I might say] that the reason people are poor here is because we need a cheap labor pool. But that's only part of the answer. I think that the inequities are built into the system. I think that some people have to remain poor so that others can become rich."

Others thought that poverty was not planned or intentionally created by the social system but was a mistake. "Poor people," said Stanley Kramer, "are the victims of a social malfunction." Still others saw poverty as the result of the aggression of individuals. Gary Marshal said, "For some people to be poor, others have to be rich. The poor are taken advantage of by the rich." Marshal did not see that as inherent in the system, however.

Most people saw the causes of poverty as inherent problems of the social system, which we would be better off without. That is, the factors that created poverty were not intentionally put there to provide cheap labor or for some other purpose, but they are there nevertheless. Lee Rich sounded a familiar note: "People are poor because of a lack of opportunity." A woman writer-producer who wished to be anonymous said, "Those who are born poor are likely to stay poor. They are doomed to repeat the poverty of their parents. Being black makes it harder, because of the visibility of being black in this country."

Douglas Benton made a similar point about immigrants and poor whites. The reason that people are poor, he said, "is that they are brought into this country without speaking the language, stacked into tenements, and they're in the same situation that other immigrants—the Russians, the Italians, the Jews, and the Irish—were in when they got here. In time, some begin to stir around, get an education, and work themselves out of their rut. The other poor are the Appalachian coal miners and farmers who have always had a marginal life. They do make a living but with only a little money. The smart ones leave. The dumb ones stay and keep trying to scratch out a living. Basically it [the reason people are poor] is lack of education, coupled with a different ethnic background, which makes it even harder to get ahead."

Stephen Kandel saw the same problems. "People are poor in America because they lack the skills and the sense of capacity which would enable them to do otherwise. An illiterate, ill-nurtured woman with no skills is going to stay poor for the rest of her life. She has no skills. She cannot compete."

Matthew Rapf saw a combination of bad luck, lack of opportunity, racism, and purposeful political exploitation as the causes of poverty. Harking back, in part, to some earlier comments on this subject, Rapf concluded his comment by saying, "The poor are kept that way because they are more easily exploited. Landlords and politicians keep them that way." This note of concern about political—as opposed to economic—exploitation was unique to Rapf.

The notion that there might be something approaching a pool of surplus labor, comprised of the "victims" of society, came from Thad Mumford. Two rather unusual views of the causes (and cures) for poverty came from Charlie Hauck and Bruce Geller." For most of the people who are born poor, the odds are stacked against them. But when anyone who was poor becomes nonpoor, you have to realize that it's not just class structure that keeps people poor. Some of it is the individual attitude that you are supposed to be poor. If a poor person has the point of view that he can overcome, he will," said Charlie Hauck. "Some of our welfare budget can be spent on fostering the attitude that people can overcome. Instead, our welfare rolls expand as our wealth expands. There is room for those poor people in the system."

Hauck's view—that some of the blame for being poor must rest on those who are poor, in terms of their own attitude toward solving that particular case of poverty—was unique. No one else attributed any of the blame for the individual's social and economic situation to the individual at all. This was extremely interesting, since the same people believed that personal exertion and cleverness could make a person rich—along with luck. In other words, there was an apparent belief that a person who was rich could largely thank himself for his riches, but a person who was poor could do no such thing. That is, a poor person was not responsible for staying poor, while a rich person was responsible, in large part, for being rich. This was yet another example of the extraordinary sympathy and compassion that TV writers and producers have for the poor.

(An anecdotal note on this line: While working in TV situation comedy and production, I saw almost unbelievable generosity toward colleagues who were down and out. Patently unqualified people were given small jobs out of anyone's way so that they would not go broke. This took money out of the producers' own pocket—and not always a trivial amount. By the same token, a prominent producer once told me that his goal, as far as becoming rich, was to be able to give $300,000 checks to charities without thinking twice.)

Bruce Geller had an even more unusual view of the causes of crime—heredity. Certain people, he believes, have innate gifts that will get them ahead. These, he said, are "alpha-people." The ones who stay poor are "beta-people." In addition, Geller said, "Society just isn't structured to make everyone get ahead."

The views of Hauck and Geller, interesting as they are,

are definitely minority views. Poor people are victims of either purposeful social behavior (the rich need the poor to be rich) or of a social malfunction far beyond their poor power to add or detract. The same kind of theorizing which lifts from criminals the burden for criminal behavior relieves poor people of the onus of their poverty. All blame is placed on society, because of either society's plotting or society's neglect.

Although this emphasis on society as opposed to the individual will be gone into at greater length, it is worth noting here that such thought might well be considered a historical artifact of socially "advanced" thinking of the 1930s or 1940s. The currents of social thought are difficult to measure, but many have written that the trend of the 1970s is in the direction Charlie Hauck mentioned— individuals taking responsibility for themselves. (Society taking responsibility and blame was much bigger forty years ago, in terms of respect and as a modish idea, than it is now. As we will see, much of the social construct of the Hollywood TV writer and producer bears the same slightly used look.) Still that was the overwhelmingly dominant concept—society as responsible for poverty— among the group studied.

But beyond social excuses, there is also a great deal of apparent and real sympathy flowing from the $5,000-a-week writer-producer to the welfare mother. There is obviously some empathetic link between the writer who earns as much as the president of a fairly large corporation and the unemployed black teenager. On the other hand, there is no empathy at all between the well-to-do producer and the head of a major oil company.

For some reason, even after achieving an extremely elevated financial status, the Hollywood TV producer-writer sees much more that is appealing and simpatico in the people far below him on the economic ladder than in those on the same step. Whether that has to do with class interest, social background, lack of comfort with wealth, or something else, I do not know. Certainly, it is not a case of the average TV writer starting out poor and remembering his humble origins. Hardly any of the writers and producers started out rich, but just about as many started out in real poverty. Whatever the reason, TV writers and producers love the poor and do not hold them accountable for their poverty. On television, this feeling takes the form of the saintly, poor, but honest folk whom anyone would trust a lot more than he would trust any rich man or businessman.

CHAPTER THIRTEEN

Clergy on Television

CLERGYMEN put in rare appearances on television during prime time. There are no regular shows that star nuns or priests or ministers at this writing. There was an attempt at a detective show starring a crime-solving rabbi, but it was cancelled after a few shows. The character of the rabbi was entirely described by the phrase "amateur detective." He had no specifically rabbinical characteristics.

Occasionally on a situation comedy we see a bumbling man of the cloth, but that, too, is rare. Recently, an episode of "Kingston: Confidential" concerned a criminal conspiracy led by a fraudulent charismatic evangelist. He was an evil, scheming man, given to lechery and bullying. Together with right-wing fanatics, he was out to take over America. That was an unusual performance, though. Usually a man of God on an adventure show is a kindly refuge from life's torments. He is the local priest to whom Baretta goes for information about a bad boy gone worse or from whom Kojak finds out a sorrowful detail about a murder victim. Almost never does a cleric play any larger role than that.

The same is true of religion in general on prime-time television. Sunday morning television is loaded with religious services, but in prime time, religion is mostly an irrelevancy, thrown in to move the plot along and with no importance one way or another. Most of the parts of religious officials could be played just as well by kindly lay men or women of a certain age. I cannot remember any recent episode in which a character was moved by religious feelings to do or not do any important act. In short, religion is something about which little interest is shown on prime-time television.

That raises an interesting question. In general, people of a liberal or left-wing persuasion might be thought of as anticlerical. Traditionally, extreme liberalism and hatred of organized religion go hand-in-hand. It is part of the whole "antiestablishment package." Yet among a group of people who have many left-wing views, I found hardly any genuine animosity toward the institution of organized religion. To some extent, this finding is reminiscent of the almost total lack of enthusiasm for government. Neither attitude is consistent with the concept of the TV writer or producer as a doctrinaire leftist.

The views of TV writers and producers toward organized religion are extremely consistent with the depiction of religion as an irrelevancy on TV. Most of those interviewed did not see religion as a significant fact in their lives or in the national life. Some saw religious fads as a worrisome or frightening sign. Some saw that for a few people the consolation of religious faith might be useful, but none saw religion as important without qualification.

The comment of Bob Weiskopf summed up the general feeling well. "I happen to feel it's not very important. If some people need it, fine. Anything that helps people in their daily lives and makes their existence more pleasant, happier, and more bearable is fine with me. I don't believe in it personally, but if it helps some people, fine."

Mort Lachman had feelings similar to Weiskopf's. "To me, it's neither negative nor positive. It's not goodness either. It's something else." Lachman did not specify what else it was.

Perhaps the most enthusiastic view of organized religion came from Gary Marshal. "I see it as a good thing. It is not working so well, but it is coming back. You need something. Those who can believe in it have a place to go." Even Marshal, however, put some distance between himself and those who were believers.

A lengthier comment about religion, which embraced most of the comments made by others and summed them up, came from Lee Rich. "Is the church important in American life? No. There seems to be a resurgence of it in a lot of young people. Young people are prone to experimenting with new things. [It was interesting to note that religion was apparently so far removed from Rich's thoughts that he considered it a "new thing."] They've gone through drugs, drinking, changes in sexual mores. Now a group are looking for religion. The church has destroyed itself over a number of years. It's no longer the church that says 'I say this and you believe.' People now question what the church says. It's being challenged. I gave up going to church at 17. I don't know anyone who goes to church.

"The church has been narrow-minded. It hasn't grown with the times. It's been lumbering along, and hasn't taken cognizance of what's going on in the world. It hasn't made the changes it's got to make. The church brought us up to believe that things were the way they made them out to be. As we've become wiser and more educated, we've started to challenge these implanted beliefs." Rich, in far greater detail, expressed the feelings of literally a dozen of his colleagues.

The woman producer who did not want her name used saw religion as a "fundamental nonissue in American life." On the other hand, looking at the specific issue of abortion, of which she is a strong supporter, she saw organized religion as "highly negative."

Stephen Kandel, whose comments tended toward the social-scientific, came out about where Gary Marshal did, in less exact phraseology. "Organized religion is responsive to a human need for certain symbolic value carriers." Kandel objected to the question as too vague and then continued, "In this secular state, religion is a valuable carrier of values, but maybe not the best kind of values. It is a cohering (sic) social structure."

Only one interviewee noted that America elected a president of immense religiosity in 1976, and that came after an expression of his own disillusion with the church. "I learned nothing about consideration in church," said William Blinn. "It was an ordeal that I put up with. Parents must instill in their kids a sense of right and wrong. That's not the church's job.

"With Carter as president—a well-liked man—(note: interview conducted in spring 1977) religion has become more important. It's not a conscious manipulation with him to promote religion, but he has a religious quality about him. But I'm suspicious when Carter says things like that he reads the Bible in Spanish to keep in touch with those people and that language. It sounds too good. It's a ploy."

Most comments, however, were far more restricted. No one else touched on religiosity as a campaign ploy, and few except those who had a particular issue about which they were concerned, such as homosexuality or abortion, expressed strong feelings one way or another. Most tended to be more like Charlie Hauck: "Organized religion is still a force in America, but I can't tell if it's good or bad."

Wherefore this lack of interest in religion, pro or con? The answer may be nothing more complex than that religion has not been a major issue dividing people of different political stripes for a long, long time. Only when religion is used as a lever to get something done—limiting the expression of homosexuality or restricting abortion— do people get concerned, at least along political lines.

It may be that since religion has ceased to play an important role in American political life, it no longer arouses opposition as business practices or expenditures on the military do. People are not concerned about harnesses or buggies either, nor about the free coinage of silver. It has been about two centuries since Jacobins identified clericialism as the enemy, and Jacobins in Mercedes convertibles now have other things to think about.

But whatever the reason for the lack of interest or feeling about religion, that lack of interest is noteworthy in itself. Certain groups in American society are extremely interested in religion and see it as vitally important. Reborn Southern Baptists are one such group. People concerned about their immortal souls—devout Catholics—are another. By definition, the people who write TV shows and produce them are not at all devout. And we can see that the significance of religion in these people's lives equals the importance it is given on prime-time television—very little.

CHAPTER FOURTEEN

The Fantasy of Life on Television

THE IMAGE of America on television is far more than a political picture alone. Television tells of life in far greater scope and particularity than simply by its attitudes toward rich or poor or criminals or military men. There is, on prime-time television, a unified picture of life in these United States that is an alternate reality.

For hours each day, people can leave the lives they are compelled to lead, lives whose limitations and frustrations hardly need to be detailed, and enter a different world that is more pleasant and less difficult in almost every way—life on television. Most TV shows are set in the present or in a time within the memory of the viewers. At the time I conducted my interviews none was in an exotic or extraordinary locale (like a space station). All of the characters are supposed to be types we are familiar with. While that familiarity may be more imaginary than real, we do see a world on television with which it is not difficult to feel a distant kinship. More than that, we see a world that is extremely appealing in a whole variety of ways. Again, these ways have to do largely with simplifi-

cation. Life on television is in many ways a schematic of
real life.

The whole alternate reality that television creates is not
a coincidence or a result of random chance. It is the product of the thinking of TV producers and writers about life.
We can see reflected on our video screens the attitudes of
TV creators. More than that, we can sense the experience
and "feel" of a city replicated on television. For what we
see on prime-time television is nothing less than the
apotheosizing of Los Angeles, and the spreading of the
Los Angeles experience across the TV screens of
America.

It is important to realize first that television is indeed
creating a unified experience, a consistent alternative
world. There is no contrast on television such as there is
between a Dostoevsky and a Gogol, between an Os-
borne and a Stoppard, between a Mailer and a Didion, or
between a Chandler and a Dunne. There is no major difference in texture or attitude between a "Baretta" and a
"Happy Days," which is to say, between a show about a
street cop in a dangerous and violent city in 1978 and a
show about an utterly happy family in a small Wisconsin
town in 1956. Both shows have the same optimistic,
cheerful attitude about life, the same utterly unshakable
premise that everything will come out right in the end, the
same absence of anxiety or worry about daily life or
death, the same feeling of life's infinite potential. With the
exception of "Mary Hartman, Mary Hartman," there is
no major show that says anything the slightest bit pessimistic about the potential for happiness of daily life.
("Mary Hartman" was not on during prime time in most
locales.) No show challenges the assumption that the un-
examined life is the only life worth living.

No show displays a kind of life that is anything but im-maculately clean and neat, in which people are anything but well-groomed and hygienic and their motivations anything but straightforward. Certainly, this has partly to do with the exigencies of a mass culture. Traditionally, the dramas of folk culture are not as complicated as those of high culture. Yet that does not account for everything. In movies (the mass culture of another era) there was dirt and tragedy and complexity, even in films with enormous appeal to mass audiences. The dirt of Tara, the sweat and grime of Scarlett O'Hara's brow, the tawdriness of John Garfield's apartment in *Body and Soul,* the grim grayness and ambiguity of fifty detective stories of the 1940s *film noir* genre are only a tiny fraction of the available evi-dence on that score.

Even in the early days of television, before it moved so completely to Los Angeles, there was complexity and sadness. When reruns of "Your Show of Shows" appear, their sad endings are almost shocking. The truly frighten-ing and earthy quality of some early "Playhouse 90" and "Kraft Theatre" shows is amazing when compared with the cheerfulness and antisepsis of the present day's fare on television.

Today's television is purer, in terms of backdrop and story endings, than the lines of a Mercedes convertible. Every day's shows bring fresh examples. Recently I saw an episode of "Charlie's Angels" about massage parlors that were really whorehouses. The three beautiful "angels" of the show were compelled to pretend they worked at massage parlors in seamy areas. (On this par-ticular show, the girls are almost always compelled to act as prostitutes or prisoners or lesbians or nymphoman-iacs.) Anyone who has ever passed by a massage parlor knows that they are invariably dirty, shabby places, with pitiful and degraded denizens. On "Charlie's Angels," the Paradise Massage Parlor compared favorably in terms of cleanliness with the surgical theater at Massachusetts General Hospital. The girls were immaculate and well-groomed, soft of speech and clear of eye and skin.

On "The Waltons," we are supposed to believe that we are in a Depression-era farming town in backwoods Virginia. Anyone who has been to a backwoods farming town in the South knows that whatever else may be said about them, they are invariably dirty and bedraggled. On "The Waltons," even the barnyard is immaculate. Marie Antoinette could not have asked for more agreeable play-farm quarters.

The grittiest TV show is generally believed to be "Baretta." Yet even there, the supposedly shabby boardinghouses are neat, bright, and cheery. Even the junkies wear fresh clothing and sport recent haircuts.

Why is television so clean? Why, when a recent show dramatized living conditions on New York's Lower East Side during the early twentieth century, did every apartment look like something that a DuPont great-grandson had recently redecorated?

The answer is simple. TV writers and producers replicate the world in which they live in their art, and the world they live in is the super-clean, super-bright world of Los Angeles, where even the slums are spotless and have palm trees in front. The world on television is the world south of the Tehachapi and north of Frontera.

Until I moved to Los Angeles, I had no idea where the images of television came from. Where on earth, I wondered, were pastel drug stores, low stucco apartments with balconies overlooking artificial waterfalls in the poor neighborhoods, and bars with almost pitch-black interiors, opening onto glaringly bright sidewalks, utterly without litter or refuse? Drive along any boulevard in Los Angeles. There is block after block of pastel drug stores and apartment houses with balconies and artificial waterfalls. Close by are the bars with pitch-black interiors.

When I lived in Washington and in New York, I wondered where in America were all cars bright and shiny, unspattered by mud, with their original colors gleaming in the sun. Where did people have new cars even if they were secretaries or rookie policemen?

In Los Angeles, where everyone spends a few hours a day in a car, everyone has a shiny new auto, even if it is a financial sacrifice. In Los Angeles, where the sun shines every day and rain never falls, cars never get muddy.

Where are policemen handsome, thin, neatly dressed and polite? They certainly were not in New York or Washington or New Haven or Santa Cruz or anywhere else except Los Angeles. In Los Angeles, the policemen look like male models, except that they do not look effeminate. They are the models for the ruggedly modish cops on a dozen TV shows.

Artists re-create their experiences, and the Los Angeles experience is one of cleanliness, brightness, shininess, and handsomeness. The artists of television do not live in drafty garrets. An artist for television simply never can experience the grittiness of daily life that might be experienced in any other city.

Among the TV writers and producers I interviewed, whenever people spoke of Los Angeles they spoke of a "fantasy land," "plastic paradise," "wonderland," "sterile concrete," "lotus land," and similar hackneyed phrases that are nevertheless accurate. The writers and

producers see and experience a life of cleanness and emphasis on good appearance that would be unbelievable
to anyone who did not live in Los Angeles. That has
become their image of life, so that when a world is re-
created on television, the Los Angeles world, the one in
the creators' minds, is the one that comes out. However
much the writers and producers may mock and decry the
sterility and cleanliness of Los Angeles, it is Los Angeles
they are broadcasting around the world as the model environment. The faces, clothes, haircuts, and cars of people on television are the faces, clothes, haircuts, and cars
of people walking down Rodeo Drive in Beverly Hills.

All of this has nothing to do with politics of left,
right, or center. It does have to do with the control that
the Los Angeles TV community has over television's content. It illustrates powerfully the influence that the experiences in the producers' and writers' minds has over what
goes out over the airwaves. Television is not creating a
world that reflects a composite of the American experience. Nor is the TV world the result of random chance.
Television is what comes out of the Los Angeles TV community's heads, and since Los Angeles is what goes into
their heads, Los Angeles is what comes out.

But this applies only to the question of appearance and
graphics. There is also a moral and philosophical world
on television, and that, too, has to come from some-
where.

Beyond the physical and visual cleanliness on television is an attitude appealing far beyond most of what real
life has to offer. On television, everything ends happily,
which might be a way of summarizing the TV climate.
There is far more, however. Every problem that comes
up on television is cured before the show is over. No one

suffers from existential terrors. They are not even hinted at.

On a smaller scale, people on television are not small-minded, nasty folks. If they are murderers, at least they are polite. No waitresses neglect to take a diner's order. No busboys spill Coca-Cola on anyone's lap. No one cuts a driver off and makes him slam on the brakes. Clerks in stores are polite and helpful. No one gets caught in traffic jams. There are no blackouts. No shopping-bag ladies, reeking of urine, stalk a traveler in a crowded subway. No snarling teenagers threaten and mock on a deserted sidewalk. Instead, people move along rapidly on highways and byways. Impediments are cleared out of the way, both visually and psychologically. At the end of 60 minutes, at the most, everything has come up roses, even if there were a few minor thorns along the way.

On television, people get things done. No one spends all day in a windowless office going over musty volumes of figures and regulations, seeking to comply with guidelines and plans laid out by persons long since dead. No one on television spends all day in bed, too lethargic or depressed to get up. On television, in fact, there is no such thing as depression. That most widespread of modern psychic ailments simply does not exist in the alternate world of television. Everyone, good or bad, is charged with energy. If someone wants to do something, he or she simply goes out and does it. There are no mental blocks working to derail the TV hero or villain.

Further, people on television think big. They are no longer concerned with telling Ricky Ricardo how much they spent on a hat. Instead, they think about making a million by selling heroin, or about ridding Los Angeles of the most vicious killer of the decade. In a comedy, a poor family thinks of getting rich. A middle-class family thinks of getting into the upper class. A black family thinks of overcoming racism. Nothing trivial occurs as a main theme any longer.

"Out there," for the folks on television, is a big world, full of possibilities. Here, a sharp distinction needs to be made between social activism and personal ambition. The people on television are never interested in social movements. They may want to be more well off themselves, but they are never interested in a political try at massive and immediate redistribution of wealth. Similarly, Edith Bunker may make a stab at social accommodation by accepting the fact that a relative is a lesbian, but she will never march for gay rights. J.J. on "Good Times" will do his best to make a killing in faulty underwear, but he will not demonstrate against double taxation of corporate dividends. Tony Baretta will extend himself to catch a murderer, but he will not agitate for a return of the death penalty. Charlie's Angels will coo with sympathy over the plight of a hooker, but they will never carry placards asking for repeal of laws against prostitution.

People on television want money and happiness for themselves. They want to be great sleuths or great criminals. But they are never interested in social movements. They have big plans and hopes for themselves, but not for society.

This entire psychic galaxy is, as far as I can tell, a reflection of the psychic makeup of the Hollywood TV producer and writer. Before I came to the world of TV production I never would have imagined that a group of people as psychologically successful and liberated as TV writers and producers existed. It is their mental world that is up there on the TV screen.

In the world of television are people who are financially successful, creative, living in comfortable surroundings, and generally quite happy. Around a successful TV production company (and the unsuccessful ones quickly vanish) there is an air of confidence and self-satisfaction that is rarely encountered anywhere else.

Those people are highly unusual folk, operating in a highly unusual milieu, and it shows. In the eighth decade of American life in the twentieth century, the working situation of Americans has become steadily more bureaucratized. Almost everyone coming out of school goes to work for a large enterprise of some kind, finding a spot on a bureaucratic ladder. The worker must flatter everyone over him and worry about everyone under him. His real rewards come not from producing anything, but from pleasing those above him on the ladder.

Workers derive their security and status from the bureaucratic structure in which they find themselves. They are cogs in a vast machinery. There is little or no creativity in their daily lives. Advancement comes with infuriating slowness. To reach a position of financial independence or modest wealth is almost impossible. Getting that extra few thousand a year in wages becomes the key goal, and few see further than that.

On the other hand, the bureaucratic structure provides a protection against having to actually produce anything. Simply serving one's time at the office is all that is required to get by. Eventually, however, that too takes its toll. The realization that one is doing nothing but serving out a life sentence results in devastating blows to one's self-esteem.

The whole process of the engorgement of institutions and the swallowing up of the individual into large enterprises leads, in my experience, to a smallness of mind. Bitterness and pettiness are generated by the unmixed frustration that is each day's portion.

Imagine, on the other hand, the world of Hollywood. It is a throwback to the world of individual entrepreneurs. Each writer sinks or swims on the basis of his product. Those people do not have to wait in a bureaucratic holding pattern all of their lives. If their product is good, they become successful and important immediately. They are not judged by how well they can accommodate themselves to a paranoid boss's suspicions. Rather, they move along or fall out depending on what they get done. They are immediately able to make themselves independent by having a skill that is in great demand and correspondingly highly paid. They float from contract to contract. Each time they begin a project, they have the opportunity to become millionaires, *and many of them do.*

The economics of TV production are such that successful writers can demand and get a proprietary interest in the shows they write. If the show is successful, the rewards become staggering. Each successful TV writer becomes an entrepreneur on some scale. The money comes pouring in. A story about Bob Dylan comes to mind. When Dylan started out, he wrote about depressed, crazy people suffering daily crises. After a few years, when his income had risen to eight figures left of the decimal point, he started to write only about happy, cheerful subjects. When asked about the change, he is reported to have said, "It's hard to be a bitter millionaire."

So it is with the people on television. They have many firm and negative opinions about various groups within the society, but they are basically fairly satisfied with life. There may be, and probably are, starving would-be TV writers in North Hollywood and Studio City who are filled with rage and anger. But the ones who have made it, the ones who are working regularly for many thousands a week, are quite content for the most part.

TV writers are not like novel or play writers. They are simply not allowed to become depressed and unproductive. They must get out a show every week. No sulking or brooding is permitted. To get out a new teleplay each week is not the pastime of blocked people. Those who sulk all day because they get a rude remark from a waiter are not successful TV writers and producers. Those who cannot drag themselves out of the house because of existential dread do not get to see their names in the credits. Life's annoyances and pitfalls are not permitted to throw the train of creation off the tracks.

Imagine, if you will, a Texas wheeler-dealer who is also able to write situation comedies and adventure shows, and there you have a good idea of the personality type of the successful TV writer and producer. He is a person who gets things done and who feels good about it. After spending years in bureaucracies of various kinds, I found it staggering to see how much each individual writer and producer got done each day. In Norman Lear's TAT Communications, there is a full-time staff of fewer than fifty to get out hundreds of millions of dollars worth of TV product. If the government had a department of TV comedy, there would be at least 75,000 employees—and they would do nothing. Naturally, each of those few people who is producing so much feels good about it and about himself. The exact opposite of small-mindedness is generated.

No one is completely or even mostly happy, but the Hollywood TV writers and producers that I met went a long way along that line. They were, and are, people who take risks and live successfully. Their horizons are broad. The small annoyances of life do not faze them unduly. They see life not as a prison sentence but as a garden of rich potentialities.

TV writers and producers are not starving in garrets, cutting off their ears to send to prostitutes. They are generally far more prosperous than the bankers they hate, far more energetic and entrepreneurial than the businessmen they hate, and infinitely more effective than the bureaucrats they tolerate. They lead fulfilled, productive lives, by most standards. They live those lives in an attractive, uncluttered world of immaculate sidewalks and gleaming new cars, pastel storefronts, and artificial waterfalls. They have been a party to striving and success in their own lives, and they have not missed the lesson of the possibilities of life. And it is this way of life that has been translated into the flickering colorful images on hundreds of millions of TV screens.

To set forth a way of life on television is not necessarily political in terms of left, right, or center. Still, it has some policy content. To replicate one's life and tell the world that it is the model of how life should be lived is a normative statement with some degree of power and forcefulness. The people who have created that model world on television are telling the rest of us—that we should try to conform to that model—implicit though the demand may be.

CHAPTER FIFTEEN

America on Television:
The Good and the Bad

———————————

AT THIS POINT, it will be helpful to summarize what the America of the TV writers and producers is, as they have told me. I asked each of the interviewees to tell me what were the three most important, in the sense of best, things about American life, and which were the three worst things about American life. In their answers one can see the clear outlines of their America. To some extent this is repetitive of earlier answers to other questions, but it serves the purpose of tying up the package.

Overwhelmingly, the best quality of American life, for the interviewees, was the opportunity for success. Bob Schiller put it in an exemplary way. "I think that probably the best thing in this country is the freedom of opportunity. . . . It isn't enjoyed by everybody because there's immobility among the poor for the most part. But still, the business of lifting yourself up by your bootstraps applies. It's easier here, I suppose, than any other place in the world, but it's still very difficult." Schiller added, "One of the best things about this country is the spirit that anything is possible. I think we're losing it, but it's something I grew up with."

Gary Marshal spoke in similarly impressive terms. "This is the land of opportunity. A man can have a shot at being anything he wants to be in America. There is a place to do everything. You may get cheated, but you can still do it."

The reticent woman producer mentioned before said, "You can still achieve the American dream, and that's the best thing to me." Stephen Kandel valued "this loose society, with its freedom of opportunity." America, he thought, still had "a feeling of the potential for an individual to make an impact on society."

It would be strange indeed if the experience of the TV writers and producers, most of whom have risen to great material success and creative power, did not contribute something to that feeling of affection for America's opportunity and, more importantly, a belief in it.

Coming next after opportunity as a best thing about America was the United States Constitution. I was actually startled by how many people spoke of their respect and appreciation for the Constitution. Stanley Kramer called it "perhaps the most fair-minded document ever written." Jim Brooks and Allen Burns saw the Constitution "as the solid foundation of a country of laws." Douglas Benton said, "It has taken the place of religion in this country. It's the one thing we hold to and believe in, and as long as we continue to do that, we'll be all right." Matthew Rapf saw "basic freedom under the Constitution" as crucial.

If freedom of speech and freedom of choice and the freedom to pursue happiness were lumped together with the Constitution, perhaps under the broad heading of freedom, that would have been a more popular "best thing" about America than its opportunity. Over and over again, TV writers and producers spoke with real feeling about their prized freedoms.

After that came a category that might loosely be called "vitality." Many people said that the energy and zest of the society were of great importance to them. Others spoke of the model way that America had mixed people of different backgrounds into a "potent brew," as the shy woman producer said.

Others spoke of the items that meant a lot to them personally. "Having some kind of vehicle" was the most important thing to Stanley Kramer. "Getting the auto club to come fix your car" was of immense significance to Gary Marshal. While these answers perhaps had some element of humor, there was possibly a hint of the vast significance of automobiles in Los Angeles in their being listed along with the Constitution in value.

For sheer plain speaking, Gary Marshal provided my favorite comment. One of the best things about America, he said, was that, "TV works. They make a lot of stuff, and everyone makes money. Possibly your mind is dulled, but everyone makes money."

Matthew Rapf saw the immense geographical diversity and splendor of America as one of its best attributes. "I love the different geographies and types of people. Maine is different from Southern California and I love that difference."

A truly staggering number of those interviewed saw Farrah Fawcett, an actress who was popular in 1977, as one of the best things about America. None meant it seriously. Several others cited the ready availability of sex.

In general, though, all of the best things mentioned by the respondents fell into the category of semialtruistic and movement-related. No one seriously said that he thought what he personally owned was of great importance. Almost everyone said that the opportunity for a hustler to get his or her fair share was enormously important. No one thought that anything he or she had done was of great importance. But almost everyone thought that the freedom to do things was crucial.

There was a heavy premium placed upon being able to do and succeed and speak one's mind in safety. TV writers and producers valued enormously the fluidity of American society. If the world is divided into those who favor contract and those who favor status, the TV writer and producer comes out foursquare on the side of those who favor contract—the ability to change one's situation by doing, taking risks, gambling.

Again, they know whereof they speak. They have advanced and prospered and reached positions of authority and power in a highly open and competitive world—that of show business creation. They prize the freedom and openness that has made that possible.

And if one looks at what the interviewees disliked, one can see the exact opposite. They disliked whatever seemed to them to narrow the possibilities for achievement and growth. They disliked what seemed to them to keep society static or stratified. Bob Weiskopf, for example, resented most "the kind of society we have here, which keeps people poor and unemployed so that others can be rich. They [the rich] use prejudice to do it, too." Whatever one may think of Weiskopf's knowledge of the potentials of different economic systems, he has in mind a system that "would give more opportunity to the masses."

Bob Schiller saw ignorance and fear as two of the worst

facts of American life. He was far from alone in his anger
at the fear that he sees as choking off growth and happiness in American life. Mort Lachman said, "I hate all the
fear in our lives. I'm supposed to be afraid of pollution, of
drought, gas shortages, cancer, everything. Paranoia is
built in."

So many people said that racism was one of the worst
things about America that, for a time, it was like hearing a
broken record. But many interviewees, black and white,
male and female, were extremely concerned about racism. Interestingly, not one person I spoke to explicitly
said that he or she thought anti-Semitism was a bad thing
about America, while many thought that antiblack feeling
was a "worst thing" and said so. This is especially intrigu-
ing because the comments of several of the producers
and writers revealed a strong sense of being persecuted
by non-Jews because they were Jewish. Leonard Goldberg, in particular, expressed a serious and graphic concern that the advertisers and network executives in
New York applied a discriminatory double standard to
Jews.

Many respondents said that materialism was one of the
worst things about America. "We tend to worship the
color television, the refrigerator, and so forth," said Jim
Brooks and Alan Burns. This comment was echoed by
many others who noted that materialism had taken hold
of them too.

Thad Mumford, though, had perhaps the most articulate statement of how freedom is restricted in America.
"The worst things about America are the lies that this
country offers. Everyone is promised a piece of the American dream, but few get it. There is a limitation of the
dream. It only applies to some. America deals with

theories and not with reality. There are built-in lies and clichés in American life."

The lacks of those freedoms for achievement and mobility that were seen as the best things were widely seen as the worst things. The TV writers and producers were deeply unhappy about anything that seemed to take away from an open society.

There was than a raft of second-order concerns scattered among the respondents. Mort Lachman was unhappy about the hydrogen bomb and the effect that it has on children. He is also angry about the change in male-female sexual roles. "Man-woman relationships are becoming steadily less pleasurable," he said. Bruce Geller agreed, seeing a problem in male-female sex-role "confusion."

Several people were unhappy about esthetic areas. One anonymous writer was furious about "a lack of taste, aesthetics, and style, as illustrated by our ugly cars, hideous houses, and ways of dressing." Stanley Kramer, too, said that "aesthetically, the American people have been robbed."

Kramer was alone in naming inflation as one of the worst things that has happened to America, which may tell something about the extent to which it affects people at his income level.

Charlie Hauck, Jim Brooks, and Allen Burns were all worried about America's self-righteousness, "our inability to perceive ourselves as others do. We make the mistake of thinking that everything we do is right."

One of the most idiosyncratic and interesting "worst things" came from Gary Marshal. "I hate the telephone company," he said. "It hurts you. I'm going to get even some day."

One of the most poignant complaints about modern life came from Lee Rich. "Life here [in America] is lonely. The loneliest I ever was, was living in New York City. You can be lonely anywhere, even within your own family."

A handful of people were concerned about America's lack of care for the elderly, and that concern seemed to cut across all lines of age.

Stephen Kandel had a series of complaints that were unique and elegantly phrased. His three worst things were: "The lack of a coherent, supportive social structure. The lack of accountability of corporations and bureaucracy and individual anomie. People refuse responsibility for the eco-social biosphere in which they live." And William Blinn saw "the McDonald's hamburger and the loss of saccharin" as two of the worst things about American life.

All of the complaints, except those about social flaws that held people back, seemed to be far less important. While writers and producers really were concerned about materialism and health care for the elderly, they were far more worried about racism, unequal distribution of wealth, lack of adequate education, and denial of opportunity. It was interesting that only one person, Charlie Hauck, even mentioned violence as a "worst thing." Apparently, the respondents did not see the fear of violence as an inhibition comparable with the "inadequacies" of the free enterprise system.

What counted to the people I talked to was the chance to make it, get ahead, and speak up, in a free and fluid society. Everything that worked against that was bad. This leads to the ever-fascinating question of why people who are so beholden to the free enterprise system and the economic opportunities it has created are so venom-

ous toward business, businessmen, and the free enterprise society generally.

There are many possible answers, some of which are
discussed in a previous chapter. But if revealed preference—what people do—is examined, we can see that TV
writers and producers certainly do not dislike the system
that has made so many of them rich. When they express
their dislike of capitalism (or our economic system, however it may be called), they are not referring to the system
that allows a producer to make $40,000 a week from a
pair of highly successful TV shows. Nor are they talking
about the possibility of an unknown writer becoming
known and rich simply on the basis of raw talent. They
are talking about what they see as the real rich in
America, the people who earn millions a year in coupons
because their grandparents were robber barons. They
have in mind people who swindle others out of large for-
tunes. They are thinking of large steel companies and
giant oil companies. In a word, they mean people who
have far larger amounts of money than most of them
(even though the writers and producers are rich by most
standards) and people who are involved in enterprises
that they see as so huge as to be beyond the law. (That is
the way they see oil companies, for instance, although
the people at the oil companies would undoubtedly see
things differently.) Further, they include people who run
enterprises that only admit white Protestants of certain
background to real authority, enterprises to which they
and their friends would never be admitted, in their belief.
What, then, is the picture of America that emerges from
our black-matrix Sonys? And why?

We see a world where everyone is comfortable and
clean, where streets and sidewalks are litter-free, where

the sun always shines. It is a place of dangerous and frightening small towns and hospitable cities. The exact opposite of what really happens is what is on television in that regard. On television, random violence never strikes in the city. Those who are killed are the victims of intricate plots, and their deaths could always have been predicted. The small town is the place where danger lurks for the innocent and unsuspecting, where corruption and evil flourish like the hibiscus in sunshine.

The world of television is peopled by killers wearing three-piece suits, heroin pushers operating behind a façade of civic responsibility, murderers of go-go dancers sitting behind massive mahogany desks in the corridors of power. Television land is a world in which the respectable pillars of society turn their daughters out to become prostitutes and heirs kill their mistresses. Businessmen make their real money by turning sweet-faced youngsters into junkies and barely pubescent girls into depraved hookers.

On television, criminals are never—literally not ever—poor, half-crazed black teenagers, operating with the knowledge that they will get only a three-month sentence for a murder. To the contrary, all crime is located in the upper strata of society on television—in the rentier class.

If, by some chance, someone other than a rentier is involved in a crime, he is innocent at heart and has been forced by poverty or demoralization into a life of crime. However, he will never, never, never be the guiding spirit or the inspiration for the crime. That comes from on high.

Police on television are brave, intelligent, hardworking, and good-looking. Only if they get in the way of a featured private detective are they officious and incompetent. Otherwise they are neatly groomed and ready to lay down their lives at an instant's notice. Only they stand between order and a chaos of executives and bankers and lawyers running berserk. They have great smiles.

Poor people on television are saintly martyrs to an unfeeling and brutal economic system. They live in immaculately neat small houses and tenements and drive smaller models of the current year's Chevrolet. They are always courteous and respectful. If they are ever suspected of crimes, one may be sure that suspicion has been wrongly flung at them by an evil and vengeful rich person. They have rich senses of humor.

Military men are either irrelevant or bad. Only on kiddie shows do they serve any useful function. Even there, they are fleshless automatons, working by the book and never doing anyone any good unless they do it by the book. If they appear elsewhere, they are corrupt Colonel Blimps or else scheming right-wing fanatics trying to take over America for the Klan.

The government on television is usually irrelevant, except that it provides meddling, harmful Drug Enforcement Agency cops who harm and balk our beloved street cops, or meddling but comical bureaucrats. People at the top of government are not shown at all except as potential targets of crazed assassins who need to be guarded by cops. The general picture of bureaucrats on television is of a far less dangerous group than, say, bankers.

Middle-class people appear generally as either heavies or fools. High-class people are always covering up for crimes against humanity.

Religion is trivial and unimportant. It occasionally moves a plot along by providing a witness or a character reference, but it rarely is more significant than that. If it is, we see it as sinister (working with the military toward a right-wing dictatorship) or hilariously hypocritical (religious figures as sex fiends).

The sum of it is that groups that might seem to some people to have leadership or power roles—businessmen, bankers, government leaders, military men, religious figures—are treated as bad or irrelevant, while underdog groups—the poor and criminals—are treated as deeply sympathetic.

It is also a world that largely inverts traditional standards of what is good or worthwhile. Education on television is absolutely valueless. Generally a highly educated man is a fool or a knave. Study or introspection is worthless. Deep thought is the villain's tool. Humility and modesty are ruses and tricks. On television, if you've got it, flaunt it. No one but a heroin dealer trying to conceal his vast and ill-gotten gains would ever live modestly. Tradition and family heritage are meaningless. They simply do not appear on television and no one ever speaks about them. Speed, action, squealing tires, and screeching brakes on Topanga Canyon Boulevard are what counts. On television everyone with money has a swimming pool and only villains have a library. Everyone has a new car, but no one knows about the laws of motion. Such is the world of television, our alternate reality, the one in which all problems are quickly resolved and in which there is no anxiety, only surcease.

As we have seen, the attitudes of the people who create television coincide almost exactly with the picture on television. TV writers and producers hate the rich businessman and love the poor criminal. They believe in the life of action and production and have no time for introspection. They love material things and hate materialism. They fear and distrust small towns and love and adore the city. They have no use for the military except as a subject of conspiracy stories and jokes. They have misgivings about some police, but basically TV writers and producers love the men in blue.

The picture of America on TV screens is the visual equivalent of what the TV writers and producers believe about the world and the televising of the way they live their lives.

CHAPTER SIXTEEN

The Sources of
Hollywood Attitudes

WHY DO TV WRITERS and producers hold the views they do? What makes them believe with such marvelous uniformity in the subjects they write about?

The answers to these questions plagued me as I compiled my research for this book. I believe that the small group of TV writers and producers is so important and has such a powerful purchase on our imaginations and minds that to find out what motivates them to hold their views would be of great value. In addition, I was curious. The people I interviewed and became friends with were fine, appealing people, and I wondered why they had views that were, frankly, much different from my own, at least when I started. Was someone missing something?

I tested many hypotheses on these TV producers and writers. Was there an ethnic bias? Perhaps, but probably not. The views I found were consistent among even the most Aryan Gentiles and the most anti-Semitic Jews. Further, some of the most extreme animus among the interviewees was directed against coreligionists.

Perhaps it was some sort of holdover from youthful flirtations with socialism. That seemed at first like a good shot. Many of the people I interviewed told me that they had been left-wingers in their youths and were quite proud of it. Some vestige of that thought probably stayed with them. Often, emotional political attachments of early years have great staying power.

But if there were vestiges of socialism, there were great hunks of capitalism. Only one man told me that he wanted to see a dramatic change in the social structure that would eliminate private property. Everyone else liked the entrepreneurial system and thrived under it. Rather, the animosity of the interviewees was directed against the largest units of capitalism and the so-called citadels of prestige and power of that system. No one wanted to lose his residuals or his points in an ongoing successful show. Everyone liked having made it up to a situation of comfort.

Was it a fad? Perhaps there was some element of fashion among the writers and producers in terms of their political beliefs. Hatred of the power centers in society might have been a trendy in-group notion that had captured the TV writing crowd just as it had captured the campuses in the 1960s. There was probably something to that, since nowhere else are fashions so quickly and thoroughly transmitted to a particular group. But that, too, was not an answer. Rather, it was a rephrasing of the question. If certain views had become the fashion, *why* had they? You could not explain it entirely in terms of imitation, since even in Hollywood, only about 80 percent of the wives carry Louis Vuitton pocketbooks, while 95 percent of the writers believed in the evil of big business. The ideas must have had some appeal beyond attempts to stay within a certain in-group.

Further, the concepts were held even by men and

women who were most determinedly unfashionable and (supposedly) anti-Hollywood. Even people who drove American-made cars believed that the military was preparing for a Fascist coup. So, while fashion had something to do with the holding of these views, it did not explain such a thorough predominance, such a strict adherence to certain stereotypical concepts.

I tried to explain the feelings of the TV people in terms of their freewheeling personalities. I tried to explain each group of feelings on each subject in terms of specifics associated with that subject—the antimilitary feeling, for instance, on the basis of lack of concern with the Soviet Union. While some answers were appealing for some questions, an overall answer that explained the animosity toward certain groups and institutions, the admiration and affection for other groups and institutions, the love of a certain free and expansive way of life, and the resentment of anything that balked that expansion—that explanation was elusive. Many things played a role—ethnicity, left-over left-wing infatuation, fashion and others. Still, there was more to it than that. To explain what it was, some anecdotes will be useful.

Soon after I arrived in Los Angeles in the summer of 1976, I dined with three important producers and their wives at the Mandarin, a restaurant in Beverly Hills. When one of the producers learned I once worked for Nixon, he wanted to know about the international conspiracy for which Nixon was a cat's-paw. What could I tell him about it? No protestations of my ignorance were adequate. Everyone knew, the producer said, to the general agreement of the party, that there was a world conspiracy of bankers and financiers and certain other people, and if I did not know it, I was a fool.

The conspiracy, according to the producer, was composed of representatives of "the eight families who rule the world." These families included the Rockefellers, the Rothschilds, the Hunts, the Pahlevis, the Krupps, the Thyssens, and others he would not name. These folks got together each year, I was told, and decided what the level of unemployment and inflation was going to be in all of the countries of the world, who would win each election of consequence, who would live and who would die, whether any wars had to be stopped or started, and so on.

As stupefied as I was to hear this talk, my dining companions were infinitely more startled to hear that I did not believe in it. They finally concluded that I, *as a traitor to my class,* must have sold out to the conspiracy and must be working for it. How else could my ignorance be explained?

When I was conducting interviews for this book, I chanced to get the views of an extremely important TV producer about a movie he had made for television. The film was about teenage prostitutes and had been a sensational success in the ratings, but it had drawn some criticism because of its sexual content. The producer's comments are beyond price: "This was a story I had read in the Sunday *New York Times.* If it's good enough for them, it's good enough for ABC. So we developed the idea into a movie for television. The censors did their things and watered it down. Then the sponsors cancelled out. They didn't want to be associated with that kind of film. I resented that. They told me, 'This is not the kind of programming our product should be shown in. We want wholesome programs.'

"These are the kinds of guys who live in restricted

communites, who are picked up in the morning by a
chauffeur, driven to Madison Avenue, drink six martinis
at lunch; probably bang some hooker in the afternoon,
go home at night, and then have the gall to cancel out this
kind of program because it doesn't suit their all-American
products. They're fucking hypocrites. During the day,
they blast the programming that's on the network. 'You
Jewboys in New York may be able to watch that stuff but
that's not good enough for my hometown.' That night at
the Playboy Club you might see the same man lying
drunk on the floor and his words lose their impact."

One of the first couples I met in Hollywood was a husband and wife who were both producers. They had
worked out an entire scenario of how the world was run.
It involved the presidents of the largest multinational corporations telling General Alexander Haig what they
wanted done. Haig, in co-operation with several ex-
Nazis, carried out their wishes. The greatest triumph of
this group, according to my friends, was to make their
own creature, a Jewish Nazi, into the Secretary of State. It
would be redundant to mention his name.

At a meeting with the head of the studio for which I
worked and several of his top producers, the subject of
wealthy businessmen came up. There was great animosity toward the heads of the large and well-known manufacturing concerns. Then someone mentioned Max Palevsky with great fondness. Palevsky, one of the richest
men in America, was a scientist who founded an elec-
tronics and computer firm and then went public. I asked
why there was such fondness for Palevsky, who was infinitely richer than the head of General Motors. With great
care, the studio head explained that Palevsky was not like
the head of General Motors. He was someone who had

started off small, who still had the heart of the people, who knew about life and suffering. Most important of all, he was someone that the studio head knew and was comfortable with. "Not some sonofabitch from Grosse Pointe," one of the producers added.

And finally, when I worked on the casting of a humorous variety show, I saw about thirty supplicants for jobs each day. Almost all of them were either Jewish or Italian, looked like it, and sounded like it. My boss kept rejecting people for "excessive Judaism" or "excessive Italianism." He explained to me that the powers that be in America want to see about them, on their televisions, people like themselves, "blond kids from Connecticut" as he put it. "Nobody wants to see these people with their New York accents, people like us," he said.

And the net result of all of it was this: The people who are in a position of creative authority in television feel very much at war with the power centers of American life, as they see them. They see the businessman class, the heir class, the military officer caste, the people from Grosse Pointe, the people in restricted communities, the people in small towns who continuously resist all the political guidance of the people in big cities, as their enemies.

Why? What has anyone in a small town ever done to the average TV producer? What has any executive of GM ever done to a $5,000-a-week writer? What has any general ever done to a man who has never been in the service, or was in the service thirty-five years ago? Obviously the animus is not personal. Yet it is powerful.

Similarly, why do the producers and writers identify strongly with underdog classes—the poor, the criminal, the black? Their daily contact with the poor is nonexistent. Most have maids, but few have much to do with them. They travel to and fro in air-conditioned bubbles and have nothing to do with the masses, as one might on a subway or a bus. No one even walks on the street in Beverly Hills or Hollywood, so there is no contact there. Yet, a bond exists between the millionaire producer and the working stiff—in the producer's mind—which does not exist between the millionaire producer and the millionaire manufacturer or heiress.

It all came together for me only by using a Marxian analysis. Although I am far from being a Marxist, I found that if I imagined the TV production community as part of a small but extremely energetic and militant class, sense could be made of everything. If the creative TV people are seen as a class that once was powerless, dominated by other classes—businessmen, heirs, and so forth—held in political thrall by an America dominated politically by small towns and their remnants, and that had then emerged into a position of power and influence, certain things became clearer.

The TV people see certain classes as their enemies from long ago. Moreover, they still see those people as enemies, except that now a sea change has occurred. Instead of having to work out of nothing to become something, the TV people are now in a position to dominate society. They can contend with the businessman class, with the military class, with small town gentry, *with anyone* for the leadership role in society.

But they realize that other power centers must be denigrated and humiliated if they are to take the top positions. They clearly see that they can still be checked to some small extent by businessmen, that the military is a closed system beyond their control, that small towns are resistant to their modish thought. So the people who make television create characters and situations that attack their class enemies, belittle different and competing ways of life, and set up their own Los Angeles style of life as the only way to go.

By the same token, they see the underclasses as their friends. They came from those classes, and if they can make them their allies in the struggles with the "sons-of-bitches from Grosse Pointe," they will have tremendous political as well as media clout. Thus there is love for police and poor people on television.

And certain groups, like clergy, are unimportant and ignored.

When the people who make television are seen in this light—as a highly articulate, well-heeled, highly motivated class on the move, eager to dominate the other powerful classes and groups in society—their entire political and social posture becomes clearer. They are doing neither more nor less than seeking to move their class to the top of the heap and to displace whatever stands in the way. By their intelligence and the power of technology, they stand astride the most powerful media instrument of all time. This tiny community in Hollywood has been given the fulcrum that can move the world—and its members know how to use it.

I do not mean to imply that the TV producers get together regularly and decide that they will attack oil companies this week and multinational extractive industries next week. The TV people have certain likes (of people who are harmless) and certain dislikes (of people and groups that are rivals), and these likes and dislikes are translated into television programming. In turn, this probably raises the public acceptance of the favored groups and the public dislike of the hated and resented groups.

Nor is this to be taken as a warning or a tocsin of alarm. No one in Hollywood seriously wants to do anything drastic to society; people are making out too well as it is. Rather, they are like newly rich dowagers. They simply want to be recognized as members of the leading stratum of society. They want their views to be looked up to. They want their way of life to be thought of as the best. They want to be unchecked and unthreatened by businessmen or others. They do not want their candidates to be beaten by rural votes. They do not want plots by military men against the free society. And so, they want their ideas of how society should be run to prevail. But those ideas are not radical or dangerous. There is no specific program. There is no threat to anyone, beyond loss of prestige. A contending power group in society, the TV people, simply wants its hour in the sun. And so TV people resent anyone, or any institutions, that compete with them. This shows on television.

For what it is worth, when I think of those people and the money and media power at their disposal, I do not see how anyone will keep them from getting their time in the sun. In fact, they probably already have it. They all have suntans. And why not? They are fine people with a great deal to recommend them. I find myself thinking more like them every passing day.

CHAPTER SEVENTEEN

The New American Culture

WHAT DOES this whole catalogue of television's content and of the minds of its producers say about American culture? To answer that, one has to go back to what America's culture was before the modern television age. America, like every country, has a folk culture. This is made up of the lore of the folk, the great mass of people, those who are not part of the more elevated areas of culture and society. Long ago, it consisted of folk tales and traditions and stories. Now, since the age of mass literacy (an age which may be coming to an end), the folk culture is largely bound up in books. It is also on display in movies, which show, by their durability and acceptance, how well they are loved by the American people.

One takes one's life in one's hands when trying to summarize the mass culture of America. There is simply too much of it and it is too varied. However, some common elements stand out. From the time of James Fenimore Cooper to the time of Joan Didion, from the lore of Thomas Jefferson to the lore of James Earl Carter, from Mark Twain to Ernest Hemingway, from Mary Pickford to Doris Day, small towns have been seen as wholesome, decent places, the wellsprings of America's best virtues. It is from small towns that innocence issues to be subverted by the city. It is from the city that corrupted innocence departs to be cleansed in small towns.

The appeal of the small town in the American heart and imagination is older than the Republic. To this day, it is used as the backdrop for commercials that want to emphasize the wholesomeness or cleanliness of a product. To this day, the president of the United States cannot get enough cornpone in his mouth when he wants to appear sincere. And to this day, while most Americans do not live in very small towns, more than half live in cities other than the largest twenty-five.

Yet the image of the small town has been frontally and continually attacked by TV culture. Television repeatedly shows the evil, conspiratorial, murderous small town, and no other, so that in the alternate world of television, "small town" and "evil" are synonymous.

This means something quite interesting and fundamental. Because the TV community is using the dominant folk culture medium of television, it might be expected to carry the message of the traditional folk culture. Far from it. Instead, the dominant folk culture medium has been captured by a group whose view of small towns is opposed to that of the folk tradition. To oversimplify somewhat, the folk culture is in service against the views of the folk, in terms of its views of small towns.

The case of businessmen is more complicated. Men of business, if thought of as robber barons of the gilded age, have never been wildly popular in American thought. Probably only a small fraction of the population ever loved the Rockefellers. On the other hand, there is a tradition of respect for the successful man of affairs. In the work of writers from Horatio Alger to F. Scott Fitzgerald to Irving Wallace, businessmen are put on show as successful achievers of the American dream, people to be envied and emulated. While the movies of Depression-era America often showed crude, rapacious business-men, they were usually foiled by more high-minded businessmen.

Certainly we can see that, on a national scale, there is more interest in becoming a sucessful businessman than a successful professor or archaeologist. At any rate, more people make the effort in business, which apparently sig-nifies something about the loathing or lack of it that Americans have for business. Even the high poobahs of government go into business as an American tradition—once they have finished their tours of duty.

So, while there is a mixture of admiration and fear sur-rounding businessmen, they are far from being univer-sally despised. Except in the works of a few reform writers like Sinclair Lewis and more notably, Upton Sinclair, businessmen are a mixed group—not all good or all bad, and certainly embodying many worthwhile character-istics. No tradition of American folk culture that I know of depicts businessmen exclusively as murderers and drug dealers and fools.

Again, as in the case of small towns, the picture that comes over the chief folk culture medium, television, is far different from the traditional folk concept. The new molder of folk wisdom, television, tells us that business-men are dangerous, homicidal frauds or buffoons. And while that is different indeed from what the tradition was before, who is to say how long any idea or concept chal-lenged so often by television can survive?

The picture of rich people in America's folk culture is slightly complicated as well. There has always been re-spect and admiration for people with old money, especially money derived from the land. Indeed, the father of our country was supposedly the richest man in the colonies. For the first several decades of national life, all of our presidents and statesmen came from moneyed backgrounds.

An image of the patrician farmer or plantation owner surveying his holdings, dispensing justice and largesse, is a fixture of folk culture. One need only think of the colonel in *Birth of a Nation* or of Scarlett O'Hara's father in *Gone With the Wind,* not to mention Ashley Wilkes in the same book and the film, to see that we have placed rich people of the land on a pedestal.

It is hard to think of any instances when rich people, as opposed to grasping people on the way up, are depicted as bad or unworthy. The picture of Lionel Barrymore nobly suffering the slings and arrows of the parvenu Wallace Beery in *Dinner At Eight* comes to mind as a model. Rock Hudson standing up for right and decency in spite of the fabulously newly rich James Dean in *Giant* is a similar ideal.

The confused but richly decent people of Henry James also appear in literature as people we might all wish to imitate, as do the characters of Marquand. On a more folksy level, we have to recall that Batman was in reality a wealthy and (seemingly) indolent young gentleman of means. Even in the early days of television, the only stupendously rich person we met, J. Beresford Tipton, who made millionaires at the wave of a hand, was a generous and kindly soul, somewhat Olympian in stature and mental bearing.

The TV picture in 1977 could hardly be more different. If J. Beresford Tipton were to reappear on "Kingston: Confidential," he would be using his money to bring about the American Reich. If Lionel Barrymore were on an episode of "Columbo," he would have killed Wallace Beery and tried to cover it up.

Whatever respect there is in the folk culture for the rich is completely and totally gone from television. "Rich" equals "murderous" in the TV world of today, or at least "rich" equals "mean" (if we are looking at a situation comedy).

Military men's role in the American folk culture is straightforward and highly complimentary. It does not take much recollection to bring out the memories of movies about great soldiers of America's past. It is even clearer in the history we all learn in school. America has no tradition of an elite and repressive military system, and we have loved our citizen soldier heroes from Mad Anthony Wayne to Douglas MacArthur and beyond. I never saw any signs on bumper stickers saying "Leave Our POWs in Hanoi." Military men are our defenders and protectors, from John Wayne to John Wayne. Except for comic sallies like *Dr. Strangelove,* attacks on military personnel as being fools and conspirators are uncommon, and, before the nuclear age, generally are unrecorded.

On television the picture, while mixed, is far more negative. On shows for children, there are still good automatons of soldiers. But when soldiers appear elsewhere, they are not the kinds of people you would want to have as close friends. Again, the medium of television is at work against the wisdom of the folk culture.

Something similar is happening in the subject areas of criminals, poor people, and religion. Americans have traditionally had little sympathy for criminals. There is no *Les Miserables* in the American folk tradition that says that the peccadilloes of criminals are caused by the relentless cruelty of society. (The movie that comes closest, *I Am A Fugitive From A Chain Gang,* is about a man who in reality committed no crime but was framed, and the literature of all countries abounds in those stories.) Criminals have been people to find out and put in jail. Yet on television, criminals are simply concealed so thoroughly that they do not appear at all except in a complete social and class disguise. (Here one enters a complex area. In certain types of middlebrow lore, crime has always involved primarily the upper classes. The novels of Arthur Conan Doyle and Agatha Christie are but two well-known examples of a vast genre. On the other hand, American movies during the Depression—the classic era of gangster movies—did show gangsters as gangsters and not as the presidents of utility companies. Thus while television's exclusive depiction of criminals as well-to-do people is not unprecedented, it is also a departure from mass culture.)

When someone is daily confronted on television with crimes committed only by men in three-piece suits and women in tennis outfits, he will eventually begin to wonder who the criminals in the real world are. And the focus of guilt may well shift from the man holding the gun to the man holding the mortgage. Against a mass medium that says that the individual criminal is not responsible for his actions, there stands a folklore that says that he is.

The question of the poor is entirely different. There, television's image has much in common with folk wisdom. Traditionally, there has been a great deal of sympathy from people who are not poor toward people who are poor—at least in folk culture. Social Darwinist thought floated through American business and universities but never made much impact on popular culture. There are endless stories about the deserving poor and very few about the people who deserve to be poor. So in that particular respect, television does not challenge the folk culture.

However, the folk culture has also traditionally placed heavy emphasis on working one's way out of the morass of poverty and into wealth and success. That is, after all, the American dream. On television, the folk idea has been changed, so that while it is good not to be poor, it is bad to be rich.

America has no established church. Even so, men of the cloth have traditionally been highly thought of in the folk culture. One need only remember Bing Crosby as the lovable Father to get the idea, while a Norman Vincent Peale or a Billy Graham would make the point even more clearly. On the other hand, leaders of sects somewhat off the beaten track, the Billy Sunday and Aimee Semple MacPherson crowd, have never lasted in public admiration. Sooner or later they become kooks and crackpots in the public mind. On television, the religious picture is mixed. There is a strain of priests and nuns who are fine, solid people. There is also a strain who are lunatic hypocritical cranks. It simply cannot be said, in this particular case, that the TV culture is at war with the folk culture.

There is a final struggle between TV and the folk culture, which is the least explicit. It is over life styles. Once upon a time there was a national legend that the best life was a quiet, unassuming one, spent in cultivating friends in a corner of the world and trying to be thrifty, considerate, and careful. Those are, in fact, widely called "the old-fashioned virtues." That whole concept is at odds with

TV life. On television, life is lived in the fast lane. The motto is to live it up, right now. Forget about quiet living. There is no wisdom in one's elders, and the past offers no guides to the present. That is the lesson of TV situation comedies and adventure shows. If you want to be cool, drive fast and speak in monosyllables, and if you hold back, you are hiding something. The new folk medium says that the old-fashioned virtues are for racists and conspirators—people who get small children hooked on drugs. Old-fashioned people are not to be trusted. The life to live, on television, is the life in Los Angeles.

To put it more clearly, if you come across someone who is full of folk wisdom and homilies, he may be: an Archie Bunker racist slob, however lovable; a con man, *à la* innumerable adventure and comedy shows; a small-town sheriff out to murder the innocent, a staple of any TV show about crime; or a fool, like the senator of "All's Fair." The good people on television are slick-looking men and women, up-to-the-minute, lithe and thin, in flashy cars and flashy clothes. The kindly housewife of Ozzie and Harriet has been utterly displaced by Farrah Fawcett.

There it is. Television shows on prime time are a new folk culture, energized by the most powerful media tool of all time, contending with the time-honored wisdom of the folk. This new folk culture is relentlessly attacking the old, not in every area, but in every area in which the TV-making class can be benefited. Against the once-mighty fortresses of the rich, small towns, and business success, the battering ram of a new and militant medium—television—has been unleashed.

It is not too early to see some of the consequences. Television, which can reverse an entire nation on a political issue of the greatest moment (who to have as president, for example) which can move a lot of soap and underarm deodorants, is at work on the national mind on a whole variety of subjects.

Already, scientists have found that the TV news, with its constant diet of sneers and negativism, makes regular viewers hostile and apathetic. What must be the views of people exposed to the far more massive doses of political and social advertising on shows that are not expressly or openly political and social? To deny that there is some effect is to deny a great deal.

However, even if the effect is difficult to measure, the effort of the TV shows and their makers is still interesting as an indication of what is on the minds of a powerful and little-known group. As I was writing this book, it became clear that Kracauer's thesis—that popular culture represents and reflects national dreams and nightmares—is untrue in the case of prime-time television. Television in this case represents nothing more than the views of a few hundred people in the western section of Los Angeles. It is a highly parochial, idiosyncratic view of the world that comes out on TV screens, the world view of a group whose moment has come.

There is no normative conclusion to this book. No plan of action is recommended. People should be free to make television as they want, in the operation of a free and open system. If those with different views want to go into TV creation, no one is stopping them. The door is not exactly wide open, but it is ajar.

It is not clear that it is good or bad that the views of the TV community get the prominent display they do. I have certain opinions, which are undoubtedly revealed in this book, but I have no overall feeling that something terrible is happening. In a free society, different groups will obtain power over different institutions at different times. Certainly the government should do nothing to stop it. But then again, no one should be stopped from pointing out what has happened in Hollywood.

INDEX

Adventure shows: businessmen on, 17–19; crime on, 38; government on, 57; pay for writers of, 83; police on, 40; poverty on, 93; producers and writers of, 11; top shows in, 7, 9–10
Esthetics, 122
Air Force, 48
Alger, Horatio, 139
"Alice" (show), 8
"All in the Family" (show), 8, 21, 74, 75, 112
"All's Fair" (show): businessmen on, 17, 20; government on, 58, 62; rich on, 82; small towns on, 64
Ambition, 112
Army, 47–48, 52, 53, 59
Artists, 90–91
Automobiles, 109, 119, 127, 131

"Baa-Baa Black Sheep" (show), 47, 49
Bad Day At Black Rock (movie), 65
Ball, Lucille, 20
"Baretta" (show), 3, 106; attitude toward life on, 108, 112; businessmen on, 17–18;

clergy on, 100; police on, 40, 46
"Barnaby Jones" (show), 9
"Barney Miller" (show), 8
Barrymore, Lionel, 141
"Batman" (show), 141
Beery, Wallace, 141
Begelman, David: on big cities, 77; on businessmen, 23; on crime, 38; on police, 44; on rich people, 85; on small towns, 69, 71
Benton, Douglas: on businessmen, 21–22; on the Constitution, 118; on crime, 38; on police, 44; on poor people, 95–96; on rich people, 87
Beverly Hills, 42, 44, 135
Bicycle Thief, The (film), x
Big cities: portrayal of, xi, 74–80, 125, 128, 134; small towns compared with, 66, 68–69
"Bionic Woman, The" (show), 47, 48, 50
Birth of a Nation (movie), 141
Blacks: crime on television and, 30–31, 34–35, 37–38, 125, 134; police and, 42; small town attitudes toward, 71
Blinn, William: on big cities, 79; on businessmen, 25; dislikes of,